Luke and the people of God

Luke and the people of God

A NEW LOOK AT LUKE-ACTS

by Jacob Jervell

Foreword by
Nils Dahl

AUGSBURG PUBLISHING HOUSE
Minneapolis, Minnesota

Luke and the People of God

A New Look at Luke-Acts

Copyright © 1972 Augsburg Publishing House

Library of Congress Catalog Card No. 72-78565

International Standard Book No. 0-8066-1232-0

Scripture quotations are from the Revised Standard Version of the Bible, copyright 1946 and 1952 by the Division of Christian Education of the National Council of Churches.

Manufactured in the United States of America

Contents

Abbreviations

AB	Anchor Bible
AnBib	Analecta biblica
ASNU	Acta seminarii neotestamentici upsaliensis
ATANT	Abhandlungen zur Theologie des Alten und Neuen Testaments
BENT	Beiträge zur Einleitung in das Neue Testament
BWANT	Beiträge zur Wissenschaft vom Alten und Neuen Testament
BZNW	Beihefte zur ZNW
CBQ	*Catholic Biblical Quarterly*
ErNT	Erläuterungen zum Neuen Testament
ET	Eglise et Theologie
EvT	*Evangelische Theologie*
FRLANT	Forschungen zur Religion und Literatur des Alten und Neuen Testaments
HKNT	Handkommentar zum Neuen Testament
HNT	Handbuch zum Neuen Testament
HTR	*Harvard Theological Review*
JTS	*Journal of Theological Studies*
LD	Lectio divina
NovT	*Novum Testamentum*
NovTSup	Novum Testamentum, Supplements
NTD	Das Neue Testament Deutsch

NTS	*New Testament Studies*
NTT	*Norsk Teologisk Tidsskrift*
RB	*Revue biblique*
REJ	*Revue des Etude Juives*
RNT	Regensburger Neues Testament
ST	*Studia theologica*
StANT	Studien zum Alten und Neuen Testament
TDNT	G. Kittel and G. Friedrich (eds.), *Theological Dictionary of the New Testament*
ThRu	*Theologische Rundschau*
TLZ-	*Theologische Literaturzeitung*
TU	Texte und Untersuchungen
WMANT	Wissenschaftliche Monographien zum Alten und Neuen Testament
ZKG	*Zeitschrift für Kirchengeschichte*
ZKT	*Zeitschrift für katholische Theologie*
ZNW	*Zeitschrift für die neutestamentliche Wissenschaft*
ZWT	*Zeitschrift für wissenschaftliche Theologie*

The transliteration of Greek words follows the form suggested by the Society of Biblical Literature. Thus *ō* is used for *omega*, *ē* for *eta*, *h* for the rough breathing, and *y* for *upsilon*, except when it is part of a diphthong (e.g. *au, eu, ui*). The letters *phi, psi, chi*, and *theta* are transliterated respectively by *ph, ps, ch*, and *th*.

Foreword

In recent decades the two volumes dedicated to Theophilus, conveniently called Luke-Acts, have been a controversial field of New Testament scholarship. The provocation came from some German professors. Ph. Vielhauer inaugurated the discussion, E. Käsemann sharpened it, and others followed up. H. Conzelmann and E. Haenchen wrote works that have already become classics. In their methodological approach all of them followed in the tracks of Martin Dibelius, who was —along with H. J. Cadbury—the great pioneer of Lukan studies in our century. Sceptical about the possibility of using Luke-Acts as a direct source of historical information about Jesus and the early church, Dibelius devoted his attention to analysis of style, of redactional reworking of traditions, and of the composition of Luke-Acts as a literary work. But most of the German scholars who devoted their interest to Luke-Acts after World War II were also influenced by Rudolph Bultmann and his program of "existential interpretation." The author of Luke-Acts was not only seen as a creative writer, but as a theologian of *Heilsgeschichte,* a representative of "Early Catholicism" within the New Testament, no longer expecting the coming of Christ in the near future and no longer able to understand the Pauline doctrine of justification by faith.

In spite of notable differences and disagreements, Conzelmann, Haenchen, and others, moved in the same general direction. Their works have set the stage for recent discussions and studies of Luke-Acts even outside Germany. Quite a number of articles, dissertations, and books have been written in which their points of view have been reviewed, criticized, modified, or rejected, in part or in total. By now, one may ask if the discussion has not been going on so long that it has reached a dead end.

In this situation, the freshness of Jacob Jervell's essays is both relieving and stimulating. They are written by a scholar who is entirely familiar with the German debate. In the 1950s he studied at the universities of Heidelberg and Götting-en. Yet, as a Scandinavian, Jervell has also been able to keep some distance from the inner-German controversies. In this book his essays will gain the wide-spread attention they deserve. Attempts to classify Jervell either among the followers or among the opponents of Conzelmann and Haenchen will prove unsatisfactory. In his methodological approach, he sides with them. But like all scholars who make an outstanding contribution, Jervell has not let his questions be determined by current opinions and controversies.

Jervell has returned to the point at which Dibelius and Cadbury started more than half a century ago: fresh analysis of the text. He has even questioned one of Dibelius' basic assumptions, that the eschatological outlook of the first Christians left little or no room for interest in stories about the spreading of the gospel and the deeds of the apostles. He tries to trace the questions that were of primary interest to the author of Luke-Acts himself. They prove to be quite different from the set of problems on which recent discussion has been concentrating. At several points, scholars in previous generations are credited with insights that have been unduly neglected in recent years. The question of whether or not Paul was to be considered a Jewish apostate is demonstrated to be a key issue. Once the central importance of the Jew-Gentile relationship is recognized, a number of other features find a natural place within a comprehensive picture.

It is not to be expected that all of Jervell's arguments will find general acceptance. But observations made and questions raised will have to be taken into account by any serious student of Luke-Acts. For that reason, I am certain that the publication of Jervell's essays will give a fresh turn to the current discussion. But the book is not addressed to fellow scholars only. The concentration on interpretation of texts within their context will also appeal to readers who care less about scholarly debate than about understanding the biblical books themselves.

NILS A. DAHL
Yale University Divinity School

Preface

In exegesis a sign of scholarship is that one never stops asking questions. This is true even in the rare cases when New Testament scholars agree. Current study of Luke-Acts seems to represent such a rare case. Scholars have attained a remarkable consensus regarding the interpretation of Luke's outlook and theology, even though there is a divergence of opinion regarding evaluation of Luke's theological contribution and his reliability as a historian.

Study of Luke-Acts in the last two decades has been dominated and inspired by outstanding German scholars like Hans Conzelmann, Ernst Haenchen, and Philipp Vielhauer. While studying in Germany I was greatly impressed by fresh interpretations of Luke's work as well as by the new methods employed by scholars following in the footsteps of Martin Dibelius. It was unfortunate that Dibelius' essays attracted little attention until decades after their publication. In his study of Acts he had made extremely valuable, creative methodological suggestions, but it was not until theology and church policy came into play that attention was focused on

13

Luke-Acts and scholarship flourished. The real inspiration came from theological controversies from new trends in theology beginning with the so-called dialectical theology, from the ecumenical movement, from the *Bekenntniskirche* and the political situation of the German churches after 1933. More and more Luke was portrayed as the representative of the institutional church, the "establishment," and as the prominent spokesman—if not the creator—of "salvation history" and a *theologia gloria.*

Despite the numerous valuable insights, principally methodological insights, I felt a growing uneasiness. It is a sound and legitimate undertaking in exegesis to allow present problems to guide one's reading of the New Testament. This often results in new observations and a more profound understanding. In the study of Luke-Acts after Dibelius this has certainly been demonstrated. But it is also difficult to avoid anachronisms. When reading current studies of Luke-Acts, I often get the feeling that the author was not a theologian writing in the second half of the first century, dealing with problems of his own time, but that he was a theologian of the Constantinian era. I get this impression principally because the "established" church that scholars assume to be present in Luke's writings could not possibly have existed in the first century; there we find nothing like an established, united church and nothing which may justifiably be called orthodoxy.

In a Norwegian church periodical in 1956 I found an essay containing some reflections about the sources and traditions in Acts, dealing with Haenchen's commentary and the source hypothesis of Dibelius. The author was my teacher at the University of Oslo, Nils Alstrup Dahl. His short article whetted my appetite for more detailed study of Luke-Acts and inspired me directly to write "The Problem of Traditions in Acts." Following Dahl's suggestions in comparing Luke with Paul, I found that in the early church conditions were favorable not only for the formation of a tradition about Jesus but also for a tradition about the apostles. This is the case because from the very outset, missionary preaching contained the following elements: the actual gospel message preached by the missionaries, mention of the missionaries who brought the gospel, and mention of people from other parts of the world who had received the gospel. The missionaries and congregations were from the very beginning part of the "gospel"; no "naked" kerygma ever existed.

All the remaining essays are concerned with the theology of Luke-Acts. In "The Divided People of God: The Restoration of Israel and Salvation for the Gentiles," I try to show that Luke never had any conception of the church as the new or true Israel. Luke is rather concerned to show that when the gospel was preached, the one people of God, Israel, was split in two. The result is that those Jews who do not accept the gospel are purged from Israel; the history of the people of God, of the one and only Israel, continues among those obedient Jews who believe in Jesus. The promises given to Israel are being fulfilled among the Jewish Christians. The initial mission to Jews was not a failure according to Luke, but a success; thousands upon thousands of Jews were converted. And these Jews bring the gospel to the Gentiles, thus fulfilling God's promises to Israel that Gentiles would join with them at the end of time.

Christians had to explain why most Jews did not accept the gospel, and this problem forms the background for the essay "The Twelve on Israel's Thrones: Luke's Understanding of the Apostolate." According to most scholars, what is behind the concept of the twelve apostles in Luke is the view of the church as the new Israel, the successor to the old people of God. Thus the Twelve are viewed as leaders of the new institution, as founders of the church's ministry, and as eyewitnesses who guarantee the accuracy of traditions about Jesus. But Luke's own view is that the Twelve are enthroned as the new leaders of Israel—there is but one!—while the old leaders are rejected because they rejected God's Messiah, Jesus. The Twelve are seen as a manifestation of God's faithfulness as he delivers and restores his people; this actually takes place in the Christian community in Jerusalem and later in the diaspora. The Twelve are not primarily eyewitnesses of the life and words of Jesus; they are witnesses to his resurrection, the interpreters of the meaning of resurrection, which Luke sees as "the hope of Israel."

"The Lost Sheep of the House of Israel: The Understanding of the Samaritans in Luke-Acts" suggests that the Samaritans are not viewed as Gentiles in Luke-Acts; they belong to Israel. In the process of Israel's restoration, which takes place among Jews who accept the gospel, the Samaritans are recalled and reincorporated into the people of God. The church that includes Samaritans is thus fully legitimate and cannot justifiably be charged with apostasy from the faith of the fathers.

"The Law in Luke-Acts" deals with a similar problem. Since Luke maintains that Jewish Christians are the only true heirs to the promises made to the fathers, he must say something about problems connected with the Mosaic Torah. In this essay Luke's highly conservative and "orthodox" view is examined. Luke is anxious to show that Jesus' followers were strict adherents to the law of Moses, and he is first and foremost interested in the ritual and ceremonial aspects of the law. By keeping the law, Jewish Christians prove they are Israel, while Gentiles, being an "associate people," are obliged to observe only those aspects of the law Moses demanded of Gentiles so that they could live among Israelites. This is the meaning of the apostolic decree.

The fifth essay is "Paul: The Teacher of Israel." Luke wrote

Acts because he was forced to do so by a crisis in the church, precipitated by rumors and controversies focusing on Paul. The problem was Paul's attitude toward the Mosaic Torah, the Jewish way of life, and Israel. Paul became a threat to Jewish Christians because he could be used against them by Jews: those who belong to the same church as Paul are apostates from the law and from scripture; they have fallen away from the people of God. Luke refutes such charges. The Paul of Acts is not the Paul of the Pauline letters but "the teacher of Israel," a Pharisee, obedient to the law, called as a missionary to Israel, not by the church, but by God himself. He is no apostate but one who teaches and preaches the hope of Israel found in the Messiah, Jesus. All accusations raised against him are false.

Finally, in "James: The Defender of Paul," the significance of the brother of the Lord in Acts is examined. James is the only undisputed authority for the author and reader of Acts, who in times of crisis provides assurance that the church is the true heir of the promises given to Israel. There is no discrepancy between the empirical church and the scriptural conception of what the restored Israel, faithful to the law, should be. Paul in particular is pronounced orthodox by the authority of James.

In all the essays the central theme is how Luke deals with ecclesiology, the question of the identity of a church which is heir to the promises given to Israel, a church which claims to be Israel and yet still includes uncircumcised Gentiles within its membership. Alienation of Jewish Christians after the influx of Gentiles into the church and rumors about Paul provide the problems Luke attempts to resolve for his readers.

I would like to extend a special word of thanks to five students from Yale University: Don Juel, the leader of the team, John Andreasen, Terry Callan, Marilyn Collins, and Ron Hock. During a seminar on Acts, they proposed that some former articles of mine be translated and published in English with additional essays representing the outcome of the studies for the seminar. They have made the translation, prepared the manuscript for publication, and read the proofs. Without them this book would not have been published.

Four of the essays in this book have previously appeared in the following journals:

"The Problem of Traditions in Acts" in *Studia Theologica* 16 (1962)

"The Divided People of God" in *Studia Theologica* 19 (1965)

"Paul: The Teacher of Israel" in *Novum Testamentum* 10 (1968)

"The Law in Luke-Acts" in *Harvard Theological Review* 64 (1971).

JACOB JERVELL

The Problem of Traditions in Acts

I

The years 1923 and 1956 are of central importance in the history of Acts research. In 1923, "Style Criticism of the Book of Acts," an essay by Martin Dibelius, appeared in a Festschrift for H. Gunkel.[1] In this essay Dibelius tried to work out an interpretation of the Acts of the Apostles along new methodological lines. Research on the Acts of the Apostles prior to Dibelius, and for the most part until the present,[2] has been especially concerned with two problems. One is the question of the use of written sources; the other is the discussion of the value and reliability of Acts as a historical source.

Dibelius used a new approach in which he tried to lay the groundwork for understanding Acts from a form critical point of view. It is most appropriate that the work of Dibelius appeared first in the Gunkel Festschrift. With his pioneering Old Testament research, Gunkel had inspired New Testament researchers to concern themselves with the small units which belong to the beginning stage of tradition and which are older than the hypothetical written sources.

19

In his well-known book *From Tradition to Gospel* (1919), Dibelius had applied these new form critical methods to synoptic research. It was his intention to get back to the literary forms and traditions within the community, which formed the basis of our present text. In his 1923 essay Dibelius applied this method to research on the Acts of the Apostles. Utilizing this approach, Dibelius continued his work on the problem of Acts until his death, and produced a series of essays.[3] But his work was not especially noticed. A decisive turning point came in 1956 when Ernst Haenchen published in the venerable Meyer Commentary Series an interpretation of Acts from the point of view which Dibelius advocated.[4]

An important thesis of this research is that circumstances were very unfavorable for the formation of a tradition about apostolic times. For Haenchen this is not a mere supposition or thesis, but rather a certainty which form critical research has established.[5] How the certainty is established is already implied in the title of one of Dibelius' essays. He himself explicitly noted that it is not by accident that he calls his essay "Style Criticism of the Book of Acts" rather than "Form Criticism of the Book of Acts," for the first result of Dibelius' new methodological beginnings was of a "negative" nature.[6] It is not really possible to work form critically with the Acts of the Apostles, at least, not in the way one can work form critically with the synoptic Gospels. In the latter, the author handed on and interpreted the forms as they arose in the tradition of the community.

Dibelius made the observation that the elements of form which were decisive for the Christian proclamation were absent in Acts. "One seeks in vain for examples fixed for preaching in the Acts of the Apostles [in question is what Dibelius called 'paradigms,' narrations which have been formed as illustrations for preaching], for there was no preaching about the apostles in the early church."[7] Haenchen says

that the preaching of the apostles was preserved neither ver-
batim nor even in its essential features by the church.[8] In
this connection he refers to the fact that not one speech of
Jesus is preserved, but only logia, individual sayings.[9] In
Acts, the logia are absent, whereas entire speeches of the
apostles are reproduced. Thus, in studying Acts, form criticism
strictly speaking cannot be employed, since the author of
Acts, in contrast to the authors of the Gospels, had before
him no material which had arisen in the course of tradition.[10]
Behind the Acts of the Apostles no community can be de-
tected, but only a man, an author.

It is impossible to be content with the mere assertion that
conditions for the formation of a tradition about apostolic
times were unfavorable. Evidence is necessary, and the following is usually given: In the time of the apostles, the words and
acts of Jesus were the object of tradition and formation;[11]
there was no place for the formation of an apostle-tradition.
The speeches of the apostles, therefore, were not transmitted.
A further consideration is the situation created by the expectation of the parousia.[12] A tradition embraces not only what
was, but also possesses a tendency toward the future, a glance
directed at what is to come. There was no interest in reports
for the coming generation during the formative years of the
church nor of the progress of mission since no new generation was expected.

If this is so, the possibilities for the formation of a tradition
are at most modest. And when the form critics weigh in the
balance the material which Luke had at his command, they
find it wanting. Luke knew a few miracle stories about the
apostles and other early Christian missionaries (e.g., 3:1-10;
5:1-11; 8:26-39; 16:25-34); in addition there were stories of
single events in the congregations (e.g., 6:8ff; 9:1-18), and
other scattered information of varying value (e.g., 1:18f; 4:36).
In the second part of Acts there is a travel narrative about

Paul's missionary journeys.[13] But these pieces of material do
not constitute a tradition. And Luke had no one who could
serve as a model.[14] Because of this the Acts of the Apostles is
to be ascribed wholly and completely to Luke himself.[15] The
speeches, the summaries, the comprehensive reports and ex-
planations, transitions in the composition, even the structure,
all of this is, to a great extent, the work of the author himself.

What we want to concern ourselves with here are not
aspects of form criticism, or better, style criticism, in and of
itself, although many of these demand comment. Neither do
we want to deal with the way in which Haenchen goes beyond Dibelius (which, by the way, is connected with the
present state of German theology), namely with the tendency
to portray Luke as a theologian with a clearly defined pro-
file. According to Haenchen, Luke advocates a theology of
glory determined by his view of salvation history, which
stands in opposition to the theology of the cross advocated
above all by Paul.

The point at issue here is the assertion that conditions
were unfavorable for the formation of a tradition about
apostolic times. Did the early church have an interest in the
activity of the apostles and the progress of mission? The
arguments which Haenchen and Dibelius offer to substantiate
their negative answer are at first glance convincing and
obvious. But they rely on nothing but probability, and only
textual analysis can give a conclusive answer. There are several
possible methodological procedures which could give such an
answer. Here we want to examine those writings in the New
Testament which come nearest to the primitive church, the
Pauline letters. "Nearest" here means nearest in time as far
as written documents are concerned.

The question is not concerned with the underlying tradition. Neither is it a question of how Luke has used such a

tradition. The problem deals rather with the formation of a tradition about apostolic times with regard to the activity of the apostles, the Jerusalem congregation, and mission. Of course it must be remembered that the Pauline letters are occasional writings which treat special problems in the congregations to which Paul wrote. These letters naturally do not contain the history of apostolic times. On no account can we expect to find abundant material. Yet it is important to examine what material there is and to learn what meaning and function it has.

II

A) Consider Rom. 1:8. This verse is in the introductory thanksgiving and prayer section. Paul thanks God because the faith of the Roman congregation is proclaimed throughout the whole world. Provisionally we will leave open whether *pistis* here means the life in faith of the congregation *(to pisteuein)* or its coming to faith *(to pisteusai)*. Neither does it make any difference how the expression "in all the world" is to be understood. The main point is that its faith is proclaimed. Here the verb *kataggellein* is used. This word is found only in Paul (7 times), and in Acts (11 times).

In Paul the word belongs strictly to kerygmatic terminology. It has the same meaning as *keryssein* and *euaggelizesthai*.[16] It refers to Christ (Phil. 1:17; Col. 1:28); the death of the Lord (1 Cor. 11:26); the gospel, the testimony *(martyrion,* 1 Cor. 2:1; 9:14). In Acts, as also in Paul, it is used as missionary terminology (e.g., 4:2; 17:23). It is possible that we have before us in this passage in Paul a weakened use of this word. With most commentators then, we would have to translate it "is spoken," "made known," "rumored," or the like.[17] In this case the statement would mean that the account of the origin of the congregation was spread like a rumor.

In any event, the language here indicates more than merely private information.

Recognition of this is in itself significant for our problem. But the weakened use of the word cannot be demonstrated elsewhere in Paul, and this translation rests completely on an inability to accept the possibility that the faith of the congregation was proclaimed. If we retain the proper meaning, we must conclude from the statement that the faith of the Roman congregation itself here constitutes the content of the kerygma. Thus the fact that a congregation is formed or exists is a subject of proclamation.

If this statement were isolated in the Pauline letters, it would be dangerous to infer too much from it. But there are other passages in the same vein. The extent to which the faith of a congregation as such can be the content of the message, can even become a word of God which is proclaimed, is more clearly stated in 1 Thess. 1:8ff. This passage also occurs in the introductory thanksgiving and prayer section (1:2-10). Paul first thanks God for the faith, love and hope of the Thessalonians (vv. 2-5). Then he states that the Thessalonians have become an example for the believers in Macedonia and Achaia (v. 7). Paul elaborates in vv. 8ff. Here he says that the word of the Lord equals the gospel sounded forth from the Thessalonians (v. 8a). Then v. 8b yields the surprising information that this "word of the Lord" is the same as the faith of the Thessalonians.

The connection between 8a and 8b presents certain grammatical difficulties. The two parts of the verse are held together by the expression *ou monon—alla*. This expression is applied only to the prepositional phrases, "in Macedonia," "everywhere." However, the two parts of the verse which constitute the statement have different subjects and likewise different predicates: 1. the word of God sounds forth, 2. your faith has become well-known, something which seems grammatically impossible. Several scholars have wanted to separate and re-word v. 8a as follows: "The word of the Lord has sounded forth from you: not only in Macedonia and Achaia, but to every place your faith has gone out." Two different things would be said in this verse, and the last part would weaken the first.[18]

We will not deal with other possible solutions here. It is most natural to assume that the two statements have the same meaning: God's word which is spread is the same as the faith of the Thessalonians. This interpretation is confirmed by what follows. Paul continues in v. 8 with the assertion that the apostles do not find it necessary to speak. They need not mention the faith of the Thessalonians because those who have received the report of this faith have themselves proclaimed it already. The content of their statement is rendered in vv. 9 and 10.

The word which describes the faith of the Thessalonians is *apaggello*. It is a (non-Pauline) typically Lukan word, used with religious as well as profane meaning. In the first case it is synonymous with *euaggelizesthai*. They do not only proclaim on behalf of the apostles about the faith of the Thessalonians, but also about the apostles themselves; when they speak of the faith of the Thessalonians, they speak about the deeds of the apostles in the Thessalonian congregations. From vv. 9 and 10 it is clear that what is proclaimed, the faith of the Thessalonians, is at the same time the content of the Christian message.

In these verses, where a report is thus given about the faith of the Thessalonians, we receive a summary of missionary proclamation. And what is proclaimed has a twofold content: we hear 1. about the coming and success of the apostles with the Thessalonians; and 2. about the faith of the Thessalonians in a) the living and true God, b) the parousia, to which a statement about the resurrection of

Jesus is also added and c) deliverance from the coming judgment of wrath through Jesus. The report of the deeds of the apostles includes a report of the acceptance of faith by the Thessalonians and also the content of this faith. This can be expressed with a slight variation in Heb. 4:2. Through faith, the word has mingled together with those who hear it. The word becomes faith and the faith becomes the word of God. This message has thus spread far beyond the boundaries of Macedonia and Achaia.

It is also important to observe the problem which has stood in the foreground of research in connection with this summary of the missionary message. The typical feature of the Pauline message is missing. There has been a tendency to explain it with hypotheses of its inauthenticity or with the assumption that we have to do with an early stage of Pauline missionary preaching. But the most obvious explanation is that here Paul reproduces the essential features of common early Christian missionary proclamation.[19] And it is very striking that this summary appears to coincide with what we know in the Acts of the Apostles as an expression of missionary preaching.

What we have found so far is confirmed in 2 Cor. 3:1-3. The problem is the letters of recommendation with which individual preachers appear.[20] Paul asserts that his letter of recommendation, which is written on his heart,[21] is the congregation (v. 2). This letter is "known and read by all men" (v. 2b). This means that everyone has heard that the Corinthian congregation came to faith through the work of Paul. Now we see in v. 3 that this letter is in reality a letter of Christ to the world, and that (there is no jump here in Paul's train of thought) it is equivalent to what stands written on the hearts of the apostles through the spirit of God, the gospel, as opposed to what is on stone tablets, namely, the law. Thus the letter of recommendation is the Pauline gospel, including the faith of the Corinthians. The gospel becomes a letter of recommendation when it is joined to faith.[22]

What *pistis* means in Rom. 1:8 and 1 Thess. 1:8 should now be clear. In 1 Thess. 1:8 it is the reception of faith by the Thessalonians which is emphasized. The same applies to v. 9: It deals with the coming of the apostle to the Thessalonians and their conversion. Thus *pistis* means *to pisteuein,* and the context of this proclamation about the faith of a congregation is the missionary work, as is clearly proved by 1 Thess. 1:6ff.

Paul was able to express these ideas in other ways which help us to understand them better. In Col. 1:4 we find again in the thanksgiving and prayer section a description of the faith of a congregation. The basis of the thanksgiving consists in what Paul learned through Epaphras about the faith and love of the Colossians (v. 8). In v. 6 it says that the gospel is bearing fruit and growing throughout the whole world (Rom. 1:8) as among the Colossians. The expression that the word of God "is growing" we know elsewhere only from Acts 6:7; 12:24; 19:20, where it means that the number of those who accept the word increases. It is easy to see how this is to be understood in our context. Paul is concerned with the faith and love of the Colossians. In 1:6c the word grows from the day the Colossians received it and came to the realization of the grace of God. God's word has a goal, that congregations appropriate it in faith and love. This goal is itself a part of the word of God. The Colossians came to faith, this faith is added to the word so to speak, and the word grows.

Also in this connection belong such statements as Paul "completes" God's word (Rom. 15:19; Col. 1:25; cf. 2 Tim. 4:17).[23] Scholars dispute the meaning of this expression.[24] But the context in which these statements occur helps determine the sense. In both places the issue is missionary work among the Gentiles. By his missionary work Paul completes the word of God. That means Gentiles come to faith. In Romans it is expressed: "so that the offering of the Gentiles may be acceptable"; in Colossians: "that we may present every man mature in Christ." When the word is received, when it causes faith and love, it becomes "complete." Paul can say the same thing about grace; it "grows" when more receive it, and it becomes empty where it is rejected (2 Cor. 4:15; 1 Cor. 15:10).

Both Col. 1:6 and 25 show that not only the reception of the word of God but also its operation in the Christian life belong to the growth of the word. That leads to new perspectives. But first, a summary: Reports of the deeds of the apostles and the faith of the congregation had their place in the life of the church, precisely in the proclamation. And it is important to note that neither legend-making nor historical-biographical, but rather kerygmatic motives were decisive.

B) And now to the further perspectives. In the opening chapter of 2 Thess., and especially in v. 4, Paul emphasizes that he boasts in the congregations of God about the faith and steadfastness of the Thessalonians in affliction. Affliction and behavior in the face of it are characterized as a public sign, a manifestation of God's judgment and redemption (cf. Phil. 1:28 and on the concept *endeigma, endeixis,* Rom. 2:15; 3:25). The fact that Paul boasts of the Christian stance of the Thessalonians means that he reports in his congregations about the Thessalonians (2 Thess. 1:4). Why? The issue here is not directly missionary proclamation, as the designation "in the churches of God" shows. It is necessary to take into consideration the many other places where Paul speaks of his boasting about his congregations. Of these we will only deal with 2 Cor. 10:12-18.

Other preachers boast of themselves before the congregations (v. 12, cf. 2 Cor. 3:1). For Paul it is otherwise (vv. 13ff.). The faithfulness of the congregation, which is therefore spoken about publicly, is God's ratification of Paul and with it, of the gospel. This faith strengthens the work of the apostle in such a way that he can extend his missionary work further (v. 14f). The commission of God to Paul is thus confirmed through the congregation's reception of the word of God. Since this reception is one of the preconditions for Paul's further work in other mission fields—in that their faith is a word of God for others—we have here a variation on the theme that God's word "grows."

But 2 Thess. 1:4 goes a step further. The issue here is the affliction of the community. In Paul the correlate to "affliction" is "consolation," and we find that the faithful behavior of a community plays an important role in Pauline statements of consolation. A congregation can here serve as a word of God. In Paul the important idea of consolation designates God's help to those who suffer. God's redeeming intervention which brings freedom from suffering is understood eschatologically throughout. "Consolation" is the gospel for suffering people. All consolation comes from God (2 Cor. 1:3ff). It springs from God's redemptive act and is connected with "salvation" and "hope" (2 Cor. 1:5; 1 Thess. 4:18; 2 Thess. 2:16; Rom. 15:4).

Consolation is thus also a form of gospel proclamation. He who is the God of all consolation can console now through the constancy in faith of a suffering congregation. It is reported in 1 Thess. 3:6, in connection with Paul's concern about the affliction of the Thessalonians, that Timothy, having been sent out, comes to Paul and proclaims (!), *euaggelisamenos,* to him the faith and love of the Thessalonians. The word *euaggelisamenos* is somewhat strange in this context. In commentaries and translations it is weakened to mean, "to bring a joyful announcement." This interpretation marks the single example of a nontechnical use of this word in Paul. But that can hardly be right. For this report is really a gospel for Paul. That is, it means in v. 7 that Paul is consoled (!) through the faith of the Thessalonians, and in v. 8 Paul adds:

"for now we live, if you stand fast in the Lord." It is God who consoles and gives life, and now the faithfulness of the Thessalonians becomes consolation.

The thought is intelligible in the light of the inner connection between apostle and congregation, a connection which puts both in Christian dependence on one another. For example 1 Thess. 2:19: the congregation is for Paul hope, joy and boasting at the parousia; 2 Cor. 1:14: on the day of the Lord the congregation is the "boast" of the apostle, as is the apostle that of the congregation; 2 Cor. 7:3: in life and death apostle and congregation are together; Phil. 2:16: that the community holds fast to the word of God is for the apostle evidence that his work has not been in vain, and that is his boast on the day of the Lord Jesus.

The statement in 1 Thess. 3:6 is not unique, as 2 Cor. 7:4-13 shows. Here also the connection "boast-consolation" is clear. Likewise here it is reported that the life of the congregation is proclaimed to Paul. And this report is God's own consolation for the apostle. It is vital for Paul to know the attitude of the congregation. The congregation confirms his apostolate and makes his gospel "grow," and Paul then makes use of it in his work in other congregations.

C) What we have discovered thus far is expressed also in the parenetic sections. We have a good example in connection with the gift to the congregation in Jerusalem. To the Corinthians Paul reports how the congregations in Macedonia behaved in this matter (2 Cor. 8:1ff). In the same way he emphasizes the good will of the Corinthians toward the congregations in Macedonia (2 Cor. 9:1ff). The purpose of these reports about congregations is to admonish the various congregations to give from full hearts. Also in this concern for *diakonia* Paul has spread "knowledge" of the various congregations, including the congregation in Jerusalem, if the other congregations did not already possess a good knowledge of the circumstances there. The theological motive underlying the admonition to give can be a reference to the Christ event; through his coming into the world he who was rich became poor, and his poverty makes many rich (2 Cor. 8:9). And in the same way it can be said of a congregation that its poverty makes many rich (2 Cor. 8:2).

At the same time deeper perspectives underlie aid for the poor. The aid appears as a proclamation of the faithful attitude of a congregation (2 Cor. 9:12ff). Through its aid, the Corinthian congregation proclaims to the congregation in Jerusalem that it is obedient to the gospel. And the aid is a sign of the fellowship of the congregations with one another.

Rom. 16:19 also belongs in this context. Paul warns the Roman church to beware of false teachers who splinter and seduce the congregation. This means that the obedience of the Roman congregation in this respect is known to all. Paul himself did not establish the congregation. Thus it is not private information about the situation of his own congregations which underlies these statements. But it is well-known to the other congregations how the Roman church has conducted itself with respect to the false teachers.

We also know from a series of statements that the apostle can use himself as an admonition, as a parenetic "word" (2 Thess. 3:7ff; Phil. 3:17; 4:9; 1 Cor. 4:17; 11:1). The conversion of the apostle is a prototype, a model according to which one is supposed to live. If one is a follower of the apostle, one is also a follower of God.[25] We have seen in 1 Thess. 1:6ff. that congregations could also be examples. Such an admonition, where the apostle depicts himself as a model for the congregation, must have had its place in the fixed instruction of the congregation. And this form of admonition can only have meaning and effect if the congregation was well informed about the deeds and life of the apostle.

III

The passages discussed up to this point show that reports of the work of the apostle, the growth and life of a congregation, and progress of mission had their place in the life of the congregation. And when one seeks out the reason for this, it very quickly becomes clear that historical and biographical interests were not decisive. It was not essentially the case that there was a desire to tell a coming generation about what had once been. Kerygmatic, parenetic interests were much more decisive. To what extent and at what moment this interest received a biographical character is not important here. However, in the foregoing little attention has been given to the Jerusalem congregation itself. But this was wholly intentional since Jerusalem did not belong to the missionary territory of Paul, and he does not write its history. Certainly there is little basis for the assumption that this congregation differed from others so that reports would not have been made about it. On the contrary, the congregation in Jerusalem had special status. The question is only whether it can be demonstrated by appeal to specific texts.

We already mentioned that the Thessalonian congregation was a model for the congregations in Macedonia and Achaia (1 Thess. 1:7). But the Thessalonian congregation is not the original model. It says in 1 Thess. 2:14 that the Thessalonians have become through their affliction, followers, imitators of the congregation in Judea.

Paul assumed that his congregations had knowledge of the persecutions to which Jews subjected the congregations in Judea. He also assumed that they knew about the relation of the Jerusalem congregation to the Jewish people. The polemic which is expressed here in vv. 15 and 16 is not anchored in the situation of the letter. It is a polemic against the Jews, and the Thessalonian congregation is not persecuted by the Jews. In this context the point is that the Thessalonians suffer under their countrymen in the same way as the Jerusalem congregation does at the hands of the Jews. This is probably a formula from the oldest Christian polemic against the Jews.[26] And this formula was thus used for congregations other than the congregation to which it properly applied. Completely apart from this, we recognize that Paul makes no comparison with any congregation.

In Rom. 15:27 Paul gives a theological argument for gathering a collection for the saints in Jerusalem. The other congregations are obliged to serve the congregation in Jerusalem in this way because they have received a share in the spiritual gifts which come from the Jerusalem congregation. What these spiritual gifts properly mean is clearly expressed in v. 28. Paul speaks here not about the congregations in Macedonia and Achaia, not about the congregations which have obtained the spiritual gifts (v. 26), but instead about "the Gentiles," by which allusion is made to the missionary proclamation. The Christian stance of his own congregations is an "inheritance" from the congregation in Jerusalem, and Paul presumes that his congregations know what he means by that.

In 1 Thess. 2:14 the "imitation" consists of the way in which the Thessalonians receive God's word. Thus God's word has gone out from Jerusalem. We have something corresponding to this in 1 Cor. 14:36. Women are told to be silent in the gathering of the congregation. If the Corinthian congregation does not conform to this, it introduces a new custom. But it has no right to do so since it is not the congregation from which God's word originally went out. That is the congregation in Jerusalem. Hence it is clear that the priority which Paul concedes to the congregation in Jerusalem (see also the following passages: 1 Cor. 16:1; 2 Cor. 8:4; 9:1, 12) is not based upon pietistic indulgence, but because God's word proceeded from this congregation. The congregation in Jerusalem makes up the "saints" as the passages mentioned indicate.

We began with the assertion that no possibility existed for a tradition of the apostles which could maintain itself alongside the tradition about Jesus. However, there is strong evidence that the Jesus tradition also contained a tradition of the apostles and the congregations. It is clear in 1 Cor. 15:3ff. This summary of the gospel, which, as Paul says, he gave to the Corinthians from the first, contains the report of Jesus' death and resurrection, but at the same time also the report of the appearance to Peter and the apostles and perhaps also to a whole list of members of the Jerusalem congregation. Paul has also told much more than this summary contains for he assumes here that Peter and the Twelve are figures familiar to the congregation. What Paul hands on is the proclamation of the Jerusalem congregation, which is at the same time a proclamation about the Jerusalem congregation. That which Paul has received from men is God's word which also speaks about men.

In no passage does Paul speak about the Jerusalem congregation and apostleship. But there is considerable evidence that he presupposes a mass of information about this congregation in his missionary territory. It comes clearly to light in the reports of Paul's struggle over the authorization of his apostleship. This whole struggle, of which we find traces in Gal. and 1 and 2 Cor., is unintelligible without the dominant position of the Jerusalem congregation. Certain suggestions must suffice.

Paul represents it as an extraordinary fact (Gal. 1:17ff) that after his conversion he did not go to the congregation in Jerusalem. The Galatians know what that means. It can in no way be interpreted as an underestimation of the original apostles. On the contrary, it is to be understood that for Paul the same authorization as an apostle is absolutely necessary for his work. Gal. 2:1ff, which contains the report of the Apostolic Council in Jerusalem, clearly presumes that the original apostles had a right to make decisions for the whole church. The purpose of the journey to Jerusalem was to obtain consent for the authorization of the Pauline gospel.

In Gal. 2:7, it looks as if the original apostles have been convinced of the legitimacy of the Pauline apostleship on the basis of what he has told them about his missionary work. Thus an acknowledgement by the older apostles was necessary for Paul. He assumes a good deal of knowledge on the part of the Galatians about Peter, whose special place as an apostle to the Jews is emphasized (2:8). Knowledge about Peter is also assumed in Gal. 2:11ff. The existence of a Cephas party in the Corinthian congregation (1 Cor. 1:12) is likewise a statement about the position which Peter held. 1 Cor. 9:3ff says that the missionary practice of Peter and that of the other apostles was known, as Gal. 1 and 2 make clear. Not only Peter, but also the other chief apostles and leaders of the Jerusalem congregation, above all the brother of the Lord, were well-known among all the congregations.

Gal. 1:23 shows that reports of the work of the apostles traveled both ways and therefore the Jerusalem congregation received reports of the progress of the missionary activity. Here it says that the congregations in Judea have learned that Paul, the former persecutor, has become a proclaimer of the faith. In conjunction with his remarks about the "superlative apostles," Paul can emphasize that the signs of an apostle also accompany his own work (2 Cor. 12:11ff, cf. Rom. 15:19). In this connection Paul uses precisely the concepts which are used in the Acts of the Apostles as signs and evidence of apostolic works: *semeia, terata, dynameis*, 2:43; 4:30; 5:12, see also 14:3 and 15:12). From this context it is quite clear that the signs of the apostle were well-known. The congregations know about the signs which legitimate the work of the first apostles, those signs which Acts reports.

IV

In the foregoing examples we have drawn on material which is important for answering our question. From it a series of other proofs could be supplied. But for us it was not necessary to set out all the material at our disposal. It was more important to achieve clarity about what function the material had. On the basis of our considerations here we can now reject as incorrect the assertion that conditions were unfavorable for the formation of a tradition about apostolic times. There was preaching about the apostles. The report of the establishment of a congregation played an important role in the missionary proclamation. Stories of the life in faith of a congregation were used in paraclesis and parenesis. A remarkable amount of information about the Jerusalem congregation was available. All of this was important to all the other congregations.

Thus the question whether conditions were favorable for the formation of a tradition about apostolic times must be answered wholly in the affirmative. This is of great importance for approaching the problem of traditions in Acts. The next step must be to determine and delimit the extent and the form of pre-Lukan tradition. Dibelius and Haenchen base their view of Luke's independent compositional activity on the lack of any prior tradition of importance, and they maintain that Luke was consequently compelled to work in a completely different way than he had done in his Gospel. With this we cannot agree. The question is rather how Luke has used the existing tradition. But that is another matter.

Notes

[1] This essay, which was first published in 1923, now appears in M. Dibelius, *Studies in the Acts of the Apostles,* trans. M. Ling (London: SCM Press, 1956) 1-25.

[2] For the most recent survey of historical-critical study on Acts see E. Haenchen, *The Acts of the Apostles,* trans. B. Noble *et. al.* (Philadelphia: Westminster Press, 1971) 14-50.

[3] The essays are collected in *Studies in the Acts of the Apostles* (see above, note 1).

[4] Already by 1959 this book appeared in a third, thoroughly revised edition. See the review by H. Conzelmann, "Geschichte, Geschichtsbild, und Geschichtsdarstellung," *TLZ* 85 (1960) 241-250.

[5] Because of extensive revisions made in subsequent editions, I have found it more convenient to retain references to Haenchen's tenth German edition. E. Haenchen, *Die Apostelgeschichte* (Meyer 3: 10th ed.; Göttingen: Vandenhoeck und Ruprecht, 1956) 95. All further references to Haenchen's commentary in this chapter will be to this edition.

[6] Dibelius, 4.

[7] Dibelius, "Zur Formgeschichte des Neuen Testaments," *ThRu* n. s. 3 (1931) 236.

[8] Haenchen, 95.

[9] *Ibid.*

[10] Dibelius, *Studies,* 2f.

[11] Haenchen, 86f. Cf. Dibelius, *Studies,* 4.

[12] Dibelius, *Studies,* 103; Haenchen, 87.

[13] Haenchen, 33f. and 95f.

[14] Dibelius, *Studies,* 3ff.

[15] Haenchen, 95ff.

[16] Cf. J. Schniewind in *TDNT* II, 707ff.

[17] See for example, O. Michel *(Der Brief an die Römer* (Meyer XIII 10th ed.; Göttingen: Vandenhoeck und Ruprecht, 1955) 37f.) where he asserts, in opposition to Lietzmann, that the word must not be weakened. He translates "is proclaimed," yet in spite of this he says in the exposition, "is made well-known."

[18] On this passage see for example, E. von Dobschütz, *Die Thessalonicherbriefe* (Meyer 10; 7th ed.; Göttingen: Vandenhoeck und Ruprecht, 1909) 69ff.

[19] See Dibelius, *An die Thessalonicher* (HNT 3; 2nd ed.; Tübingen: J. C. B. Mohr (Paul Siebeck), 1925) 6. The reason must be sought in the fact "that Paul here, as in the following section, revives the recollection of the missionary work in Thessalonica. In missionary work he seems to have used more traditional Christian ideas and concepts and thus to have spoken more like any other Christian missionary than we perceive from his four main letters."

[20] It cannot be established with certainty who these opponents of Paul are or where they received their letters of recommendation. We accept the old explanation as most probable: they are Judaizers and appear with letters from circles within the primitive congregation at Jerusalem. It is certain, as we can gather from the Corinthian letters themselves, that the opponents have given Paul considerable difficulties in his relation with the congregation at Corinth. That is understandable if they, with or without justification, were able to appear with the authority of the Jerusalem congregation in Pauline missionary territory. This is also evidence that Paul's congregation must have had considerable knowledge of the Jerusalem congregation.

[21] It says literally: *en kardias hēmōn* where Paul speaks of himself and Timothy. Nearly all textual witnesses have this reading, whereas Sinaiticus and a few other later witnesses read *hymōn*. This reading seems to go back to v. 3 where it is said that the apostle's letter of recommendation is written in the commission of Christ, while one imagines that Paul has written this on the hearts of the congregation.

[22] Commentators have argued that in v. 3 Paul is no longer speaking of the letter of recommendation, but proceeds to speak of the gospel. But the thought is that Paul knows no other letter of recommendation than the gospel and ranks his opponents' letters of authorization alongside the tablets of the law. This is also to be explained from the wish of his opponents, namely, that the Christians in Corinth should live according to the law of Moses. See my book *Imago Dei* (FRLANT 58; Göttingen: Vandenhoeck und Ruprecht, 1960) 178f.

[23] *Plēroō*, must not be understood here from the synoptic statements about the fulfillment of the word of God, as Lohmeyer proposes; see his *Die Brief an die Kolosser und an Philemon* (Meyer 9: Göttingen: Vandenhoeck und Ruprecht, 1953) 81. In question are the many passages in the synoptics where divine promises and predictions, mostly in scriptural quotations, are fulfilled since what was predicted has happened. Here the passive form is almost always used.

[24] According to A. Schlatter, *Gottes Gerechtigkeit: Ein Kommentar zum Römerbrief* (Stuttgart: Calwer Verlag, 1935) 387f., the expression *plērōsai ton logon* means that concrete effects on the bearers follow the proclamation; according to O. Moe, *Brevet til Romerne* (Oslo: Aschehoug, 1948) 548, it means that the proclamation of the gospel of Christ is accomplished through Paul's deeds. R. Asting, in *Die Verkundigung des Wortes im Urchristentum* (Stuttgart: W. Kohlhammer, 1939) 138, says that when Paul brings the revelation to Gentiles, this part of the word of God is fulfilled—the redemption of the Gentiles. Lohmeyer, 80: "Fulfillment gives to its purely religious character historical reality; what was from of old only spoken by God in Christ becomes event through the work of the apostles." Cremer-Kögel, Michel, Bauer, Delling *et. al.* conceive the expression geographically. Paul proclaims the gospel in the whole Mediterranean territory.

[25] See my book, *Imago Dei*, 195f.

[26] Cf. Dibelius, *Thess.*, 11.

The Divided People of God

The Restoration of Israel
and Salvation
for the Gentiles

I

Why does the church carry on the Gentile mission, and how has it come about? It was a major concern of Luke[1] to answer these questions in Acts.[2] Different interpretations of Luke's explanation of the Gentile mission have been made by scholars. To be sure, we have become more careful with references to Luke's universalism. The Lukan account of the Christian message can no longer justifiably be interpreted to mean that the primitive Christian proclamation was directed to all peoples without regard for the special position of Israel within the history of salvation.[3] The interpretation of Luke's theology of mission most widely advocated today may be described as follows: Luke describes the rejection of the Christian proclamation on the part of the Jewish people. Only after and because Israel has rejected the gospel, and for that reason has itself been rejected, do the missionaries turn to Gentiles. Because of the behavior of Israel, the Gentile mission was set free, so that precisely the Jewish rejection of the missionary message proved to be the decisive presupposition for the Gentile mission.

41

At first, the focus was exclusively on the mission to Jews.[4] Ernst Haenchen[5] describes the situation as follows: According to Luke, the leaders of the primitive Christian mission were Jews who were faithful to the law and who did not originally intend to undertake any Gentile mission. They were, however, driven irresistably to it by God himself.[6] This was the basic theme to which Luke added auxiliary motifs.[7] The missionaries addressed Gentiles only after the Jews had rejected the gospel. If at the time of Luke the church carried on the Gentile mission exclusively, it is because Israel has rejected the gospel and therefore has been rejected by God. Further, God is not partial when he grants salvation to peoples other than Israel.[8]

It emerges from Acts that the promises fulfilled in Christ[9] belong to Israel and that a share in these promises is given to Gentiles.[10] Because Luke presents the Jews as rejected, he must, in order to carry through this scheme, understand the Christian church as the true or new Israel in contrast to the "empirical" Israel, which Haenchen finds "sharply laid out" in Acts 3:23.[11] In what follows the question that concerns us is how Luke motivates the Gentile mission theologically, not how the origin of the Gentile mission is to be understood historically. We advance the following theses:

(1) Luke does not describe a Jewish people who, as a whole, reject the early Christian message, and in which the believing Jews are exceptions. The numerous references to mass conversions of Jews, on the one hand, and the narratives about the rejection of the message, as well as the persecutions incited by Jews, on the other hand, show us that the missionary proclamation has divided Israel into two groups: the repentant and the unrepentant.

(2) In Acts, "Israel" continues to refer to the Jewish people, characterized as a people of repentant (i.e., Christian) and

obdurate Jews. The Gentiles are the non-Jewish peoples. A necessary process in salvation history begins with missionary work namely, the exclusion of the unbelieving, unrepentant Jews from Israel. The portion of Jews who believe in the Messiah and are willing to repent appears as the purified, restored, and true Israel. "Israel" does not refer to a church that is made up of Jews and Gentiles, but to the repentant portion of the "empirical" Israel; they are Jews who have accepted the gospel, to whom and for whom the promises have been fulfilled. For Luke this relationship is the presupposition for the Gentiles' sharing in the promises. According to Luke, the church has not separated itself from Israel, nor has it gone beyond the boundaries of Judaism. Rather, the unrepentant portion of the people has forfeited its membership in the people of God.

(3) From the beginning of the mission it is certain that according to Scripture and in agreement with the missionary command, the Gentiles have a share in salvation. Sharing in salvation, however, means having a share in the promises of Israel. Thus, the mission to Gentiles is fulfillment of Scripture in the sense that the promises must first be fulfilled to Israel before Gentiles can share in salvation. This fulfillment has occurred in the conversion of repentant Jews. Thus, the presupposition does not consist in Israel's rejection *en bloc* of the gospel, since thereby a Gentile mission would no longer be possible for Luke because then salvation would not come from Israel as Scripture prophesied. The mission to Jews is a necessary stage through which the history of salvation must pass in order that salvation might proceed from the restored Israel to the Gentiles. In the process of following through consistently what is sketched above, Luke describes how the preaching to Jews also includes mention of the Gentiles' sharing in salvation, while the basic proclamation to Gentiles emphasizes the fulfillment of the promises to Israel.

II

The common opinion that Luke describes the Jews as a whole as rejecting the gospel conflicts with the striking remarks in Acts that relate the great success of the Christian mission to Jews.[12] Mass conversions of Jews are again and again reported: 2:41 (47); 4:4; 5:14; 6:1, 7; 9:42; 12:24; 13:43; 14:1; 17:10ff.; (19:20); 21:20. It can hardly be disputed that these remarks derive from Luke, or that he used them systematically with a purpose in mind.[13] He distributes them carefully throughout his account, and they fulfill a definite function in his composition.

These remarks are understood by most commentators as an expression of the divine blessing that rests upon the church.[14] This understanding is possible and even probable. Yet if one proceeds from the viewpoint that Israel as a whole rejected the missionary preaching, then it seems very remarkable that the divine blessing is shown precisely in the mass conversions of Jews. Several observations, however, make it probable that the manifestation of the divine blessing upon the church is hardly the main concern of the author, but is at most a peripheral concern.

What is characteristic of these remarks is that they, as already mentioned, are concerned with mass conversions of Jews and that Luke is less concerned to narrate the conversion of Gentiles with the aid of such remarks. The latter also occur, though less often, at 11:21, 24; 14:1; 17:4; 18:8. Another observation should be made in this regard. The references to the conversion of Gentiles speak mainly of "God-fearing" Gentiles, who already are related to Israel and Judaism *via* the synagogue, though without being circumcized (13:43; 14:1; 17:4, 12). The passages show that Jewish and Gentile conversions have been so combined that both groups accept the gospel together.

Already in the Cornelius narrative (10:1ff.), in which the conversion of God-fearing Gentiles has primary significance, the "Jewish" piety of Cornelius is emphasized and underscored. Where the Christian missionaries preach to "pure" Gentiles, i.e., to those who are in no way related to Israel, no accounts of mass conversions are found. If it is the intention of Luke to describe the divine blessing on the missionary preaching, this blessing does not follow the church everywhere. The main concerns for Luke are: (a) to narrate that tens of thousands of pious Jews have become believers (21:20)[15] and (b) to show that the converted Gentiles were "God-fearers," i.e., men who were previously related to Israel. The Gentiles of the synagogue accept the gospel.

A difference in these remarks in the first and second halves of Acts is also to be noted. Up to the Cornelius story and the Apostolic Council related to it, the remarks have a peculiar character as compared to the later ones. In the first half of Acts these remarks are so ordered and constructed that one cannot change their sequence without sacrificing their meaning. They are not stereotyped and schematic, as in the latter half, i.e., after the Cornelius story. We see that their construction reveals a clear progression: in 2:41, 3,000 Jews are converted; in 4:4 there are 5,000;[16] in 5:14 still more are added than before,[17] great numbers of women and men; in 6:7 the number is increased enormously. Already here Luke anticipates the statement in 21:20: there are myriads, tens of thousands, of believing Jews.

Luke's concern, however, is not primarily to prepare for his statement in 21:20, but to set up some presuppositions for the beginning of the Gentile mission. It is evident furthermore that Luke intends to show that the mass conversions have taken place in Jerusalem. The purposeful and parallel construction of reports about the conversions is related to the significance of Jerusalem for Israel, the believing as well as the obdurate. When James in 21:20 speaks of tens of thousands of believing Jews in the church, he is talking about Jerusalem, as is clear from v. 22. The expressions that characterize this intense growth are linked with the center of Israel in which the gospel celebrates its greatest triumphs. Thus, it is clear that when the gospel finally moved beyond Jerusalem to the first Gentiles, a significant number of believing Jews, a large part of Israel, had already accepted the gospel.

The reports of conversions outside Jerusalem, about Jews as well as Gentiles, are thoroughly stereotyped: "many," "not a few," "a crowd," etc. Here no inner relationship between the reports exists. For Luke it is more important to show the growth of the church up to the beginning of the Gentile mission than to expound the later missionary successes. In the Jerusalem period of the church nothing seems to fail for the missionaries when the goal is winning Jews for the gospel. Only the leaders of the Jews, or at least some of them, reject the message. After the beginning of the Gentile mission the success is more capricious. Nevertheless, it is typical that almost everywhere in the diaspora great crowds of synagogue Jews are converted.

It is also to be noted that it is those Jews who are faithful to the law, the real Jews, the most Jewish Jews, that become believers. The first mass conversion takes place among the devout (2:41; cf. 2:5); a great number of the Jerusalem priests become believers (6:7); the "noble" Jews are faithful to the Scriptures, and these are the ones who are converted (17:11ff.); a ruler of a synagogue accepts the gospel (18:8); 21:20 is typical for Acts as a whole: tens of thousands of Jews who have become believers are all zealous for the law.

Hand in hand with these reports of conversions in Acts are accounts of opposition that the missionaries encounter, principally from Jews. To be sure, Luke knows that the Gentiles themselves are closed-minded regarding the gospel; yet this interests him less because this does not have the same theological significance as does the rejection on the part of Jews. From his striking juxtaposition of conversion and opposition it is clear that Luke does not simply want to express the divine blessing on the church by accounts of mass conversions.

The reports of conversion and opposition have to do with Jews. There is an interplay here between rejection and acceptance of the gospel by Jews. This relationship can be demonstrated for Acts as a whole.

First, the Jerusalem scenes: The consequences of Peter's speech at the temple (3:11-26) are—(a) persecution of the missionaries by the Jewish leaders (4:1ff.) and (b) at the same time a mass conversion (4:4). Strangely, this passage seems to have been spliced together, assuming that it is the intention of the author to set conversion over against persecution. Before the second trial and imprisonment (5:17ff.) Luke again mentions the overwhelming growth of the community (5:14); again we see how awkwardly this verse is placed in the context since it breaks up the clear connection between vv. 13 and 15 and occasions a contradiction between vv. 13 and 14. It appears, however, to be the purpose of v. 14 to show that despite the caution of some Jews, great crowds have been converted. Before the execution of Stephen and the resulting persecution, Luke reports of the success of the mission, especially among the Jerusalem priests (6:7).[18]

It can be argued that these reports of conversions in the first half of Acts were necessary to depict the development and growth of the community. The same picture is also found in the synagogue scenes of the diaspora in the second half of Acts. Here as well, Luke cannot be content with a picture of Jewish rejection and opposition. The appearance of the missionaries in Pisidian Antioch results first of all in Jewish conversions and only then in opposition (13:42f., 45).[19] In Iconium Jews and others become believers, while the unrepentant

Jews incite persecution (14:2ff.). In Thessalonica some Jews are converted, while others begin a new persecution (17:5f.). A report of a mass conversion of Jews in Beroea, who received the missionaries with open minds, is followed by a description of an incitement of the population by Jews from Thessalonica (17:12).

If we go through the whole list of reports, we usually find the same pattern: conversion and opposition, which turns into persecution. So far as these reports of opposition are concerned, it is also characteristic that the beginnings of the Gentile mission mark a shift in the account. In the Jerusalem period some of the leaders of the Jews, especially the Sadducees, whose orthodoxy Luke questions, are generally described as opponents (4:1ff.; 5:17ff.; 6:8ff.), while the people and many priests are either converted or well disposed toward the church (2:47; 4:21; 6:7). In the second half of Acts, which deals with the behavior of the Jews of the diaspora, the account is somewhat different. A portion of the Jews rejects the gospel, suggesting that the Jews of the diaspora emerge as opponents to a greater extent than the Jews in Jerusalem. It is important for Luke to emphasize that the Christian mission was especially successful in Jerusalem, while the gathering of Jews of the diaspora does not have the same significance, although this also belongs to the fulfillment of the promises.

Through this pairing of mass conversions and opposition an important fact is expressed. Luke does not describe a picture of the Jewish people who *en bloc* have rejected the gospel, which would itself occasion the Gentile mission. It is likewise not correct, in referring to Luke's point of view, to say that the overwhelming majority of Jews have opposed the message. That this is the case historically is not debated here where we are exclusively concerned with Luke's understanding. What Luke makes clear to his readers is the following: From the beginning the mission to Jews was successful, so that a significant portion of the Jews was converted. There were already "many tens of thousands who were zealous for the law" before the church undertook the Gentile mission. After the way to the Gentiles was opened the success among the Jews continued. The church appeared as a church of Jews first and then of Gentiles. The rising opposition from the Jews is connected with this.[20]

Luke also recognizes a Gentile reluctance and hostility, but this interests him less. Above all, he wants to describe what happened to Israel through the Christian missionary preaching. The picture is clear: Israel has not rejected the gospel, but has become divided over the issue. With the coming of the gospel to Rome the message is preached to the Jews of the whole world. And the last picture of the Jewish people in Acts is a picture of an Israel divided over the mission: some are convinced, others remain unbelieving (28:24f.).[21]

III

What does the division within Israel mean for Luke's understanding of the Gentile mission? In Luke's writings "Israel" always refers to the Jewish people. At no time does it serve to characterize the church, i.e., it is never used as a technical term for the Christian gathering of Jews and Gentiles. It is also clear that *ta ethnē* nowhere means the non-Christian world, but only the non-Jewish peoples.[22] The early catholic understanding of the church as a *tertium genus* in relation to Jews and Gentiles and ultimately as the *new* Israel that is made up of Gentiles and Jews is not present in Acts. Luke's view is different: The "empirical" Israel is composed of two groups, the repentant (i.e., Christian) and the obdurate. It is important for Luke to show that the Jewish Christian church is a part of Israel.

This is expressed in a variety of ways. Luke emphasizes that the earliest Jerusalem Christians live as pious Jews; the believers frequent the temple, live in strictest observance of the law and in accordance with the customs of the fathers, precisely because they hope for the restoration of Israel (1:6; 2:46; 3:1; 5:12; 10:9ff.; 11:2; 15:1ff.; 16:3; 21:20ff.; etc.). Paul is persecuted by Jews, not because he advocated something new in relation to Judaism, but because, according to Luke, the basis of Paul's message is the heart of Jewish belief, the resurrection (23:6; 24:15, 21; 26:6f., 27; 28:20). Whether this was really the case does not matter. For Luke the Christian missionaries represent what is truly Jewish, and they lay claim to be the true representatives of Israel.

The Jewish Christians in the diaspora, the Jews who have been won for the gospel, do not emerge as an independent group (19:8ff.; 26:11). That salvation belongs to Israel, and indeed to the empirical Israel, need not be verified. The consciousness of being Israel and the connection with the only Israel that Luke knows are reflected in Luke's use of the address *andres adelphoi*. This address is not restricted to the Christian community.[23] Luke does call Christians "brothers;" this use, however, is not the most typical usage for Luke. It is characteristic that the author uses this form throughout Acts as a Jewish address. On the other hand, the address "brothers" for Gentiles is consistently avoided (2:29, 37; 7:2; 13:26, 38; [15:7, 13]; 22:1; 23:1, 6; 28:17).

A typical example of Luke's usage occurs in 13:26. Paul's speech in the synagogue of Pisidian Antioch has a two-fold address: "Brethren, sons of the family of Abraham, and those among you that fear God," that is, the God-fearing Gentiles present with the Jews in the synagogue. The same double address is found in v. 16: "Men of Israel and you that fear God." The designation "brothers" is more than a polite address and can, as the cited passages demonstrate, be applied only to Israelites. Thereby the solidarity and inner connection in the people of God is expressed. To be a brother means to belong to the family of Abraham, to share in the promises. *Adelphos* means Israelite (thus: 1:16; 3:12, 17; 7:23, 25f.; 13:26).

This term is not reserved for the Christian church; in fact, such a use is not especially frequent in Acts. In contrast, it is emphasized that the Jewish Christian missionaries use this address for Israel and thus they acknowledge that they belong to Israel. At least they claim the right to represent this Israel.

The picture of the Jewish orthodoxy of the Jerusalem church and the remarks about the mass conversions in the first half of Acts are closely related for Luke. The author sketches a picture of Israel for whom the promises are fulfilled; he does not show us a new Israel arising out of the rejection of the old, but he speaks of the old Israel for whom the promises are fulfilled, since a great portion of the people has been converted. Thus, Luke prepares for the Cornelius story as well as for the Apostolic Council. The account of the Apostolic Council contains an explanation of the Cornelius story in the speech of James (15:13-21). This speech makes quite clear what Luke intends in reporting about mass conversions and the Jewish orthodoxy of the Jerusalem church (15:16-17). Here Amos 9:11 is cited, according to the Septuagint (influenced by Jer. 12:15). This section of Acts 15 says:

16. After this I will return, and I will rebuild the dwelling of David, which has fallen; I will rebuild its ruins, and I will set it up,

17. that the rest of men may seek the Lord, and all the Gentiles who are called by my name,

18. says the Lord, who has made these things known from of old.

This rendering of Amos seems to mean that God will first rebuild and restore Israel, and then, as a result of this event, the Gentiles will seek the Lord.[24] We can at least infer from the text that the Cornelius story is cited as proof that the restoration of the fallen house of David has already occurred, as well as the Gentiles' seeking the Lord. We must still determine what "the restoration of the fallen house of David" means. Haenchen, who emphasizes that one must find a meaning that fits Luke's theology, thinks that v. 16 expresses "the story of Jesus that culminates in the resurrection." Thereby the promise given to David is fulfilled, and this fulfillment through the resurrection causes the Gentiles to seek the Lord.[25]

For this interpretation one must recognize that the quotation, if one assumes that Luke is speaking here, is not well chosen. The connection between vv. 16 and 17 is broken; v. 17 emphasizes "the rest of men" and "the Gentiles," which presupposes that the first half of the quotation alludes to Jews. But in Haenchen's interpretation, the first half of the quotation has no relevance. Obviously, one cannot expect too much logic in the use of Old Testament quotations in New Testament writings. Nevertheless, methodologically one must ask which understanding corresponds to Luke's overall scheme, and above all how the quotation fits in the context. The connection should be clear. Here Luke is not concerned with the position of the Gentiles with respect to the history of Jesus, nor with the Gentile mission in general, but with the law-free Gentile mission (15:1ff., 19ff.).

Corresponding to the two groups in the quotation, the concern is with the two groups of men, precisely because the problem in the preceding account involves the relationship between believing Jews and converted Gentiles (vv. 8ff.). The two allusions to the Cornelius narrative make this clear (vv. 7, 14). If the passage is concerned with the relations between Jews and Gentiles with respect to salvation, then the quotation fits admirably with his scheme of "Jew first" and, as a result, the Gentiles, the rest of men. It appears that in the context the use of the quotation can mean nothing other than the restoration of the people of Israel, that is, of the old Israel. If this is the case, then Luke has James express a very old conception of mission—the conversion of the Gentiles is the fulfillment of the promises to Israel.[26] This should not be understood to mean that the promises given to Israel have been transferred to the Gentiles, while Israel has been excluded, but that the Gentiles have gained a share in what has been given to Israel. This fits with Jewish expectation, that at the end of times the Gentiles will be included in the restored Israel.

How does this fit with peculiarly Lukan conceptions? First of all, it accords well with the mass conversions of Jews and the orthodoxy of the Jerusalem community, the function of which we can now appreciate. James' speech, which presupposes a restoration of Israel, is in keeping with Luke's notion that the repentant, believing Jews are the true Israel. According to Luke, v. 16 refers to this group. The promises have been fulfilled, not only by the resurrection of Jesus but also by the acceptance of salvation by a significant portion of Israel. Before the Gentiles were included, great numbers of Jews were converted. The mass conversions of these Jews appear consistently before the Cornelius story and the Apostolic Council, which in turn presupposes the addition of a number of Gentiles, which is what Luke describes after the conversion of Cornelius.

The gospel has indeed come from Israel, from the people of God, and the promises have thereby been fulfilled in that Gentiles have been joined to the Israel that has accepted salvation.[27] Thus, the continuity of salvation history has also been insured; Luke is unaware of a break in salvation history. The point of view "Israel first and after that the Gentiles" is, therefore, not to be understood as an unsuccessful proclamation to Jews, which thereby compelled the proclamation to Gentiles so that Gentiles form a substitute for the lost people of God. The continuity of salvation history does not lie exclusively in the history of Jesus but also in the people who represent Israel.

Luke is also aware of Jewish opposition to the missionaries

and their message. But for him this opposition is not a representative expression of the attitude of Israel toward the gospel. Those circles out of which the opposition arises are not the legitimate representatives of the people of God. Although the church of Luke's time, and the greater portion of the tradition handed down to him, spoke of a total rejection of the gospel by Jews, Luke's point was that only part of the people had rejected the message.

This partial rejection raises a problem that Luke handles in the second speech of Peter (3:11-26, especially v. 23). With a quotation from Deuteronomy 18 Luke speaks of Jesus as a prophet whose mission to the people Moses had prophesied. This means that anyone who has not heeded the prophet's words should be rooted out from the people. The last words of the quotation, those about the purging, do not belong to the text of Deuteronomy, but are added from elsewhere. This shows how important this part of the statement is for Luke. According to the context the "people" can only be the "empirical" Israel. The rejection of the missionary preaching, which Peter prophesied, is to result in the purging of the unrepentant portion of the people from Israel.[28]

A Gentile Christianity that claims to be the true Israel in contrast to the "empirical" Israel is not described at all by Luke. The unrepentant are therefore not excluded from the church which includes both Jews and Gentiles, but from the "empirical" Israel which is made up of believing Jews. One may not therefore characterize the Lukan picture in such a way that the church has transgressed the boundaries of Judaism, but that a portion of Israel has forfeited its right to belong to the people of God. What has happened as a result of the missionary preaching, namely, the exclusion of the unrepentant, signifies the fulfillment of the prophetic words of 3:23.

A conversion of all Israel was not a problem for Luke because it is God's will that some should be excluded. According to Luke, James can rightly say that the conversion and restoration of Israel can be the basis for the Gentiles' seeking the Lord. This is the case with Cornelius. And so it happens later that the missionaries are found in synagogues with their mixed audiences. It is therefore correct to emphasize that conversion occurs *via* the synagogues because the scattered of the diaspora are gathered and because the exclusion of the unrepentant must take place here. Thus, according to Luke, James can assert what he does with complete justification. Countless Jews have been converted—and here we come to the third important factor in the reports of conversion. One cannot doubt the real orthodoxy of these converted Jews: All are zealous for the law.

An essential Lukan presupposition for the Gentile mission now becomes evident. One usually understands the situation to imply that only when the Jews have rejected the gospel is the way opened to Gentiles.[29] It is more correct to say that only when Israel has accepted the gospel can the way to Gentiles be opened. The acceptance of the message took place primarily through the Jewish Christian community in Jerusalem. The unrepentant portion of the people cannot hinder the fulfillment of the promises to Israel. In fact, the opposition is the fulfillment of prophecy. Even the streaming in of Gentiles, described in Acts as mass conversions in connection with Jewish conversions, reveals who really belongs to Israel.

When Peter speaks to Cornelius and his household, he represents Israel. That is supported by the mass conversions in Jerusalem. It is underscored by his reluctance as a Jew to associate with a Gentile (10:9ff., 34f.), and finally by means of his speech containing the gospel that has been sent to Israel. That Cornelius seeks out Peter shows the actual inclusion of Gentiles.

IV

For Luke, the Gentiles' sharing in the promises to Israel is not only a historically necessary event connected with the Jewish rejection of the gospel. The missionary preaching to Gentiles is commanded by God in Scripture (Luke 24:47;[30] Acts 3:25; 13:47; 15:16f.; cf. 10:43). As is well-known, the initial mission is described in Acts as a mission to Jews, and the admission of Gentiles begins in principle with the conversion and baptism of Cornelius. It is clearly stated that Gentiles are to be included when the missionaries preach to Jews. Nevertheless, Gentiles do not appear until the restoration of Israel and the fulfillment of the promises to the people of God have occurred. This is made clear in several ways.

According to Luke 24:45ff., the resurrected Lord himself revealed to the apostles the key to understanding the Scriptures. The Scriptures witness to the crucifixion and the resurrection of the Messiah *and* "that repentance and forgiveness of sins should be preached in his name to all nations, beginning from Jerusalem." *Ta ethnē,* as is evident in Acts, are the non-Jewish peoples. What goes out from Jerusalem is the proclamation for the peoples. Even if the missionaries turn to Jews, the Gentile mission must also begin at the same time.

The mission solely to Jews does not mean a restriction of salvation to Israel, but that the peoples must be reached through Israel. The command to world mission is repeated without scriptural proof in 1:8: The apostles are to be witnesses in Jerusalem, Judea, Samaria and to the ends of the earth. According to Luke, the apostles clearly understood that they were called and commanded to world mission. On the surface it may appear inconsistent that the apostles carry out the mission exclusively to Jews;[31] but this expresses Luke's understanding of mission. It is striking that the apostles emphasize in their speeches to Jews the sharing of the Gentiles in salvation, while they mention in their speeches to Gentiles their commission to Israel.

Let us look first at the speech of Peter at the house of Cornelius (10:34-43). The apparent lack of connection between the situation and the sermon has often been mentioned.[32] The introductory statement of vv. 34f.—"that God shows no partiality, but in every nation anyone who fears him and does what is right is acceptable to him"—shows that the occasion is significant for the history of mission. The rest of the speech, which is the essential body of the sermon, however, makes no reference to this situation. "In contrast, the Jesus event is described as taking place solely within a Jewish framework; and in 10:42 the 'people' to whom the resurrected one has commanded the witnesses to preach is doubtless the Jewish people."[33] In other words, in this extremely important speech to Gentiles Peter discusses the salvation that has come to Israel.

Since Peter speaks precisely in this context about the commission of missionaries to Jews, we can understand the speech only to mean that the message to Israel also includes Gentiles who can be reached only through Israel. For it is said to Israel that Jesus is the Lord of all (v. 36)[34] and the judge of the living and the dead (v. 43).[35] When Cornelius attains salvation, the promise that through Israel the entire world attains salvation has been fulfilled.

One problem arises however. According to Luke, God must compel Peter to seek out Cornelius and thus God himself initiates the Gentile mission.[36] But it is striking that the address of the gospel to all people is repeatedly directed to Jews. In Peter's speech to Jews from all over the world (2:14-40), at which representatives of Jews living among all peoples are present (2:5),[37] Peter says that the promise is "to you and to your children and to all that are far off" (2:39). The quotation from Joel 3:5 in Acts 2:21 is taken up again here, and in light of Luke 24:47 and Acts 1:8 the passage can only be understood as the inclusion of Gentiles in the promises to Israel.[38] Obviously, "all that are far off" can also mean Jews who are far off, and such a double meaning may be intended. Through Judaism, through Israel, Gentiles are to be reached. This is significant because the audience represents all peoples. Because of the mass conversion of diaspora Jews, the Jerusalem community is composed of Jews from all peoples.

The speech of Peter in 3:11-26 concludes with a discussion about the meaning of the Jewish decision for or against the call to repentance. The last statement of this missionary sermon to Jews contains a hint that the message has a further objective beyond the Jews (v. 26): to you *first* it has been preached.[39] What Luke has Peter say is noteworthy. Before God instituted the Gentile mission through the Cornelius event, before the Jews had the possibility of rejecting the gospel, Peter knew of the acceptance of Gentiles.

What purpose does the reference to the salvation of Gentiles serve in this context? The double possibility of the Jewish people is delineated in vv. 22-26. Not to be converted means being excluded from the people (v. 25). Conversion means a share in the messianic salvation and a share in the covenant of Abraham (vv. 25f.). To be sure, the listeners, as Jews, are already sons of the covenant of Abraham (v. 25a), and thus salvation means a ratification of this covenant for those who have been converted and have not been excluded from the people. This covenant is described by means of a quotation from Gen. 22:18: ". . . and by your descendants *(sperma)* shall all the nations of the earth bless themselves." This seems to express the same thought as 15:16ff.: through the conversion of Israel the peoples are to be blessed. Do we find here the concept of the addition of Gentiles as a part of the fulfillment of the promises to Israel?[40] Thus, does salvation come through Israel? Or must one interpret the passage to mean that the Jews are to be blessed in Christ, the descendant of

Abraham? [41] According to this interpretation, the Jews would not be the descendants of Abraham, but could become his descendants through Christ. The issue can only be settled by determining what *to sperma* means, Christ or Israel.[42]

In Luke's writings the expression "seed of Abraham" never refers to Christ or the church; in 7:5-6, and also Luke 1:55, "the seed" is Israel (see also Luke 13:16; 19:9); according to Acts 13:23, Jesus is *apo tou spermatos,* where *sperma* again means Israel. The word and its equivalents refer only to Israel and Israelites.

Decisive, however, is the way both interpretations fit in this context. The Scripture quotation is not intended to point out that Israel is the family of Abraham, but it is intended to clarify the covenant with Abraham which states that all peoples are to be blessed in Abraham's seed. If this seed is Christ, then the following meaning results: the Jews are the sons of the covenant and of the prophets; they are now all to be blessed through the seed of Abraham, i.e., through the proclamation about Christ. Then, however, v. 26a is without reference, and it is not understandable why the Gentiles suddenly are designated by the use of *prōton,* "first"; moreover, the expression "the families of the earth" is artificial. It also seems peculiar to find Christ represented here as the one descendant of Abraham, whereas just before the Jews are referred to as the descendants of the patriarchs. For the reader "the families of the earth" must have referred exclusively to Gentiles.

Verse 26, however, demands a reference to Gentiles in the quotation in v. 25 that provides its motivation. Thus, "seed" means Israel, and "the families of the earth" means the other peoples of the earth. So understood the context is clear. Verse 23 speaks about the exclusion of the unrepentant, whereas v. 25 works out what should occur to those who remain a part of the people, that is, the restoration that has been determined from of old. This is a condition for the coming of the Messiah (v.

20). Restoration also means the restoration of the people, and if "seed" means "Israel," then this meaning follows: through Israel, through the sons of the prophets and of the covenant, the other peoples of the world are to be blessed. Therefore, God sent Christ first to Jews with the intention of reaching Gentiles through them.

The addition of Gentiles is part of the restoration of Israel. The ambiguity of "the families" has a clear meaning, provided that we keep in mind that the "seed" is made up of the repentant portion of the people, the Jewish Christians. Salvation, which originated with Israel, is given to all that are far off, Jews and Gentiles, as is expressed by the two-fold mass conversions of Jews and God-fearers.[43] So understood, this speech prepares for the Gentile mission that is later described and that is intended according to v. 26.

Similarly, the speech of Paul to the Jews of Pisidian Antioch (13:16ff.) is important for understanding the Gentile mission. It is emphasized repeatedly that the promises belong to Jews and that salvation has been sent to them (vv. 23, 26, 31, 33). But it is said to Jews that everyone who believes in Christ is justified (v. 39; cf. 10:43, in which the same thing is said to Gentiles). The reader could understand v. 39 only to mean that justification also includes Gentiles, who share in salvation. This is confirmed by the warning that concludes the speech (vv. 40f.). Hab. 1:5 is cited according to the Septuagint in which a reference is made to a future act of God. This act, according to vv. 46ff., is the preaching to Gentiles of the gospel that really belongs to Israel.

The speech achieves a two-fold result: a great number of Jews and proselytes are converted (v. 43), while others reject the gospel (v. 46). This rejection and the warning in vv. 40f. are usually understood to mean that when the audience does not accept the gospel, the gospel is preached to Gentiles.[44] The Gentile mission thus appears to be the result of Jewish disobedience, which seems to be confirmed by v. 46: "Since you thrust it [God's word] from you, and judge yourselves unworthy of eternal life, behold, we turn to the Gentiles."

In the first place, v. 47 speaks against this interpretation. The Gentile mission is justified by a reference to prophecy (Isa. 49:6): "For so the Lord has commanded us. . . ." Thus, even before the speech in this synagogue, the missionaries were under command to turn to Gentiles. The partial rejection on the part of the Jews does not provide the basis for preaching to Gentiles because the Gentile mission is already contained in the missionary command of God. Sent to Gentiles, the missionaries turn, because of the command of God (v. 46), to Jews! The meaning is clear, provided the object of the quotation from Scripture is Israel, which is to be set as a light to Gentiles, and provided the missionaries represent Israel. Through them the light is brought into the world of the Gentiles.

Nevertheless, the disobedient among the people must first be purged so that it becomes clear who belongs to Israel. This is the significance of the warning in vv. 40f. Obviously, it does not mean that the Jews should be on their guard lest the gospel go over to Gentiles, but that they should be on guard lest they despise the future act of God, the sharing with the Gentiles in the "property" of Israel; otherwise, the Jews themselves would be purged from the people. The sense of v. 46 is: Because you have made up your mind and have judged yourselves unworthy of the salvation of Israel, the time has come, since we are obeying God's command to Israel, to offer a share in salvation to Gentiles.

The episode in Pisidian Antioch raises the following question: Why does Luke, despite the declaration of the missionaries in 13:46 that they are now going to Gentiles, go on to describe their preaching in synagogues (14:1; 17:1, 10, 17; 18:4, 19, 26; 19:8)? It is conceivable that the scene in 13:44ff. represents a typical incident. The decision in Antioch is repre-

sentative for all later decisions regarding the Jews.[45] Nevertheless, Luke emphasizes that the unrepentant must be excluded
from Israel and that the repentant must be gathered before
the Gentile mission is possible.

If this is taken into consideration, then the question must be
answered differently. For a reference only to the Antioch incident overlooks the variations in the synagogue scenes. Luke
holds the reader in suspense from scene to scene in order to
show the different reactions to the preaching. At certain places
the missionaries are received cordially (e.g., 17:10ff. and
18:19f.); only at one place do we find obstinate rejection
(18:4ff.). It is clear, however, that Luke wants to point out
that some of the "genuine" Jews here are also believers (v. 8).

It is typical for almost all the scenes that the Jews become
divided into two camps over the missionary preaching during
which the unrepentant are separated from the others. If one
begins with this division, then one can call the incident in
Antioch a typical event. The function of the continued preaching in the synagogues becomes clear only in view of the principle that whoever is not converted will be purged from the
people. The events in the synagogues stand out not only as
typical incidents; they also represent events that are necessary
to clarify who belongs to Israel. According to Luke, one cannot be purged from the people vicariously. The decision in
v. 46 is to be taken strictly only for those in Pisidian Antioch.
It is therefore not the intention of Luke to show how God
has won a people for his name from Gentiles in place of an
Israel that has rejected the gospel. Rather, the influx of Gentiles occurs because the promises to Israel have been fulfilled.[46]
According to Luke, one finds repentant Jews, who make up
the true Israel, wherever the gospel is preached. Israel is present not only in Jerusalem, but also in the diaspora.

The synagogue scenes extend throughout Acts, even up to its
conclusion in Rome. This conclusion is also characteristic

(28:23ff.). Once more we find the familiar picture of some believing, others unbelieving (v. 24). Thus, Acts closes with a description of a people divided over the Christian message. The question may be asked whether *epeithonto* is to be understood as describing the conversion of individual Jews only.[47] If it is really Luke's intention to describe the complete rejection of the gospel on the part of the Jews, then it is very strange that he seems to emphasize clearly the division among the Jews and appears to speak about the unbelief of only a portion of the Roman Jewish community. But if one compares v. 24 with the other accounts of Jewish behavior, it becomes clear that Luke describes, once more and conclusively, the division with Judaism. To the unbelieving portion Paul, in vv. 26f., applies Isa. 6:9f. as a judgment on the hardened. These last words can not refer to those mentioned in v. 24.

Accordingly, v. 28 says: "Let it be known to you then that this salvation of God has been sent to the Gentiles; they will listen." We note that the verb is an aorist, *apestalē*. The salvation of God does not come to Gentiles for the first time, that is, as a consequence of the Jews' rejection. It had already been given to them in the past. Long ago, when the missionaries were addressing Israel, the place of Gentiles in God's plan of salvation was clear. When Paul says that the Gentiles will listen, this implies an "in spite of"—in spite of the partial rejection on the part of the Jews, the gospel and thereby the sharing in the promises of Israel are to be offered to Gentiles.

In Rome the gospel has reached the ends of the earth (1:8). It is an open question whether Luke is of the opinion that with the work of the apostles and of Paul the world mission was already completed. Nevertheless, 28:28b seems to point to the time of the author, since the Gentile mission is really only beginning. With the account of Paul's stay in Rome, however, he has also brought to a close the mission to the Jews. In the course of the account in Acts Luke is little concerned to show the development of the mission to Gentiles.[48] He leads his readers to the threshold of the Gentile mission. His major concern is to narrate what happened before the initiation of the world mission. Scripture has been fulfilled in that the promises made to the people of God were given to Gentiles. This has not occurred in such a way that they have been transferred from the Jews to the Gentiles but that they have come to the Gentiles through the repentant Israel.

This is why Luke attaches such great importance to the description of the fate of the gospel among the Jews as a division that must take place so that the promises could be fulfilled. If his account has led to Rome, the situation is explained in this way: Everywhere in the world, from Jerusalem to Rome, the gospel was preached and the purging of the unrepentant Jews was proclaimed. Jews all over the world know the gospel, and with the conclusion of Acts there is also the conclusion of the mission to Jews.

Strictly speaking, Luke has excluded the possibility of a further mission to Jews for the church of his time because the judgment by and on the Jews has been irrevocably passed. A conversion of the entire Jewish people by the Gentiles in the future, as Paul envisions in Rom. 9-11, is out of the question for Luke. His understanding of the history of mission forms a decisive obstacle. The unbelieving portion of the people is rejected for all times, and to those who have been converted the promises have been fulfilled. They are the cornerstone of the true Israel into which the Gentiles have now been incorporated.

V

According to the preceding discussion an important question must be answered. If it was clear from the beginning in the preaching to the Jews that the Gentiles should also share in the salvation of Israel, how then is the Cornelius event (10:1—

11:18) to be understood? Does not this narrative imply that the apostles had not engaged in a mission to the Gentiles at the beginning? [49] God himself must compel Peter to seek out Cornelius, which overcomes the reluctance of the apostle and which leads the missionaries finally to understand that God also wills salvation of Gentiles. Only then—or so it seems— does the breakthrough to the Gentile mission come. In any case, it is clear that the conversion of Cornelius is not described as a consequence of the rejection of the gospel on the part of the Jews. Nevertheless, it seems that in this report the apostles were not clear beforehand that the gospel should also be offered to Gentiles. If we understand it in this way, then we are led into great difficulties by the earlier statements in Acts that claim that the Gentiles should be added *via* Israel.[50] These statements would suggest that the Cornelius story does not narrate the basic decision that includes the Gentiles in the sharing in salvation. Here the question is: In what way and at what time do the Gentiles receive a share in the promises to Israel?

In the account of the Apostolic Council in Jerusalem (15:1-35), the Cornelius incident functions as a proof (vv. 6f.). This incident has a definite influence on deciding the question of the Gentile Christians' freedom from the law. The problem is not the Gentiles' sharing in salvation, but in what way they should receive salvation. This is precisely what the Cornelius story is to clarify. In v. 11 Luke expresses what Peter has learned from the Cornelius event: the Gentiles will be saved "just as they [the Jews] will." Serving as a proof for this is the statement in v. 9, which says that God bestows the gift of the Spirit to Gentiles in the same way as to believing Jews. As a substitute for Jewish membership in the people of God, God accepts as valid the cleansing that has come upon them by faith (v. 9b).

Thus, the new thing is not the salvation of the Gentiles, but that they are saved simply as Gentiles without circumcision and the law, without first becoming proselytes. That does not mean the annulment of the privileged position or the mediating role of Israel, as the speech of James shows with its quotation from Amos 9:11f. (vv. 13ff.). The speech presupposes the connection with Israel, though without the Jewish form of observance of the law and without Jewish status. In any case, the addition of Gentiles through the restoration of Israel is presupposed.[51] Therefore, Peter *must* institute the Gentile mission in his role as the representative of Israel. The question discussed at the Apostolic Council is primarily the circumcision of Gentiles and not the Gentile mission as such. Is the Cornelius story also to be understood in this way?

Usually, the narrative is understood as having two themes that are inseparable—the question of associating with Gentiles, i.e., table fellowship between Jews and Gentiles, and the problem of the admission of Gentiles into the church. In the Lukan composition all the stress is put on the latter.[52] Luke wants to say that the idea of the Gentile mission stems neither from Peter nor from Paul, but from God.[53] Methodologically, it is correct to look for Luke's intentions primarily in the repetition of the Cornelius story (11:1-18).[54] What is new in relation to the earlier chapters in Acts is not the "idea of Gentile mission" or that the Gentiles now come to share in salvation, but that they are admitted as Gentiles, as uncircumsized.[55] Luke expresses this repeatedly.

The Jerusalem critics of Peter do not direct their criticism against the Gentiles' sharing in salvation; this is simply stated (11:1). On the contrary, the rebuke is made that Peter has gone to uncircumsized persons, conversed and eaten with them (11:2)[56]—so also 10:28 in the interpretation of the vision (10:9-16). Peter's vision allows what the law forbids, fellowship with Gentiles, because God has given them a new status and has declared them clean (11:9; 10:15, 28; 15:9). This is a renewal of the Torah. Nevertheless, what is essential is that God has given Gentiles the gift of salvation, the Spirit (11:17; 10:44ff.).

Thus, the main point is that salvation has come to the Gentiles through Israel, and has come in such a way that the Gentiles do not need circumcision in order to be justified. At this stage of the account Luke requires no divine revelation in order to maintain that the Gentiles should share in salvation. A divine revelation, however, is necessary at this moment in order to develop the thought that Gentiles are saved without circumcision and belong from now on to Israel. Thus, Luke preserves the continuity of salvation history and the mediating position of Israel; he maintains the fulfillment of the promises to the "empirical" Israel, and he is able, moreover, to proclaim the right of Gentiles to salvation without circumcision. He draws the following conclusion from the Cornelius story (11:18): "Then to the Gentiles also God has granted repentance unto life," i.e., as Gentiles.

The brothers who are zealous for circumcision (15:1) do not question the free access of Gentiles to salvation, but question only their admission without circumcision. Now we can see how Luke has understood the earlier attitude of the apostles toward Gentiles. In order not to jeopardize their Jewishness he permits them to be of the opinion that "Jewish" salvation will come to Gentiles if they are circumcized. God, however, has decreed by means of a heavenly pronouncement that Gentiles are to be saved from now on without circumcision, and thus has instituted the new form of the Gentile mission. The Gentiles, however, are not Israel, but have been associated with Israel, for which reason circumcision remains for Jews.

VI

Because the promises that were fulfilled in Christ belong to Israel, and because Luke knows only one Israel, i.e., the Jewish people, the Gentile mission forms a difficult problem for him. He was not acquainted with the later solution of this difficulty by means of the conception of the church as the new Israel made up of Jews and Gentiles; and this hardly fits with his view of history. At the time of Luke there was no longer a mission to Jews, though the church was greatly concerned about the Gentiles.[57] How can the church justify its neglect of the Jewish mission while it preaches the Messiah of Israel? Is not the church compelled to concern itself with Jews? Luke's solution is that the apostles have completed the mission to Jews. They have gathered the repentant Israel and have given to Gentiles a share in the salvation that comes from the repentant people of God. The conversion of Gentiles is itself a fulfillment of the promises to Israel so that the apostolic mission to Jews turns out indirectly to be the Gentile mission. After the completion of the mission to Jews, the time of the Gentile mission, as predetermined in the history of salvation, began; and this is the time of Luke. In this way Luke is able to explain why there still is an Israel alongside and unrelated to the Christian church, to which the church is not obligated. The reason is that this Israel includes the Jews who were excluded from the people of God on account of their rejection of the gospel and who have no right to the name "Israel." At the same time, Luke is able to maintain that Israel is really the Jewish people, namely, the repentant ones, the Jewish Christians who formed the nucleus of the apostolic church. These Jewish Christians were the historically necessary transition to a predominantly Gentile Christian church. In these Jewish Christians the unity and continuity of salvation history were evident. Gentiles received a share in the promises of

this Israel. It is also settled that there can be no talk about a
renewed mission to Jews without misunderstanding the work
of the apostles and without calling into question the right of
Gentiles to the promises. For only through Israel's acceptance
of the gospel has access to salvation become a reality for Gentiles.

Notes

[1] The question of authorship is not discussed here. Thus, "Luke"
does not refer to an identifiable author.

[2] See especially J. Dupont, "Le Salut des Gentils et la Signification
Theologique du Livre des Actes," *NTS* 6 (1960) 132-155, and E.
Haenchen, *The Acts of the Apostles: A Commentary,* trans. B. Noble
et. al. (Philadelphia: Westminster Press, 1971) 100.

[3] Concerning Lukan "universalism": E. Lohmeyer, *Galiläa und
Jerusalem* (FRLANT 34; Göttingen: Vandenhoeck und Ruprecht, 1936)
44f.; N. Q. King, "The 'Universalism' of the Third Gospel," *TU* 73
(Berlin: Akademie Verlag, 1959) 199-205.

[4] Three passages in particular, namely, 13:46; 18:6; 28:28, give rise
to the claim that Luke understands the rejection of the gospel on the
part of the Jews as the decisive presupposition of the Gentile mission.
Among the recent studies see Haenchen; H. Conzelmann, *Die Apostelgeschichte* (HNT; Tübingen: J. C. B. Mohr (Paul Siebeck), 1963);
and F. F. Bruce, *The Acts of the Apostles* (Grand Rapids, Mich.:
Eerdmans, 1953). Further: F. Hahn, *Mission in the New Testament,*
trans. F. Clarke (London: SCM Press, 1965) 134; J. C. O'Neill, *The
Theology of Acts in Its Historical Setting* (London: S. P. C. K., 1961)
70, 82f.; U. Wilckens, *Die Missionsreden der Apostelgeschichte*
(WMANT; Neukirchen: Kreis Moers, 1961) 50ff., 70ff.; Schlier, "Die
Entscheidung für die Heidenmission in der Urchristenheit," *Die Zeit der
Kirche* (Freiburg: Herder Verlag, 1956) 94ff. Schlier, however, is not
concerned specifically with Luke's theology.

[5] Haenchen, 100ff.

[6] Haenchen's presentation at this point does not seem altogether
clear. Nevertheless, the statements on p. 100 are probably to be understood to mean that a proclamation to Gentiles by the apostles
seemed impossible because of their Jewish faith: ". . . the instigators

and leaders of the Christian mission, far from falling away from their Jewish faith, in fact held fast to it . . . but God (!) unmistakably and irresistibly steered them into the mission to the Gentiles."

[7] *Ibid.*

[8] According to Haenchen, this way of thinking is characteristic of Luke and Gentile Christianity of his time. Therefore, Haenchen must use the term "auxiliary theme," for this theme is hardly compatible with the other, being especially inappropriate for the first-mentioned motif. The presupposition must then be that the leaders of the primitive Christian mission have come gradually to the understanding that God wanted to give the message of salvation to Gentiles as well. Concerning other themes, see p. 101. According to Haenchen, proof from Scripture is also an auxiliary idea. Proof from Scripture can be understood only as ancillary, for this theme also fits badly with the first-mentioned idea: the Jewishness of the primitive community that precluded any Gentile mission. If Luke has, in general, reflected upon these different themes, then the idea must be that the apostles have gained the understanding gradually that the Scriptures also pointed clearly to the Gentile mission. But this can hardly be compatible with the sources, being particularly inappropriate for the immense significance of scriptural proofs for the understanding of the admission of Gentiles to salvation (thus already Luke 24:46f.).

[9] Concerning Luke's development of the theme of promise-fulfillment see E. Lohse, "Lukas als Theologe der Heilsgeschichte," *EvT* 14 (1954) 256-275; Paul Schubert, "The Structure and Significance of Luke 24," *Neutestamentliche Studien für Rudolf Bultmann* (BZNW 21; Berlin: A. Töpelmann, 1954) 165-186.

[10] See, e.g., 2:39; 3:25; 13:47;—Luke 2:24-32.

[11] Haenchen, 209; cf. also H. Conzelmann, *The Theology of St. Luke,* trans. G. Buswell (New York: Harper & Row, 1960) 152ff. For another view, N. A. Dahl, "A People for His Name," *NTS* 4 (1957-58) esp. 324.

[12] It is not explicitly mentioned that the mission is to Jews; but in the structure of Acts it can hardly be understood otherwise because the Gentile mission begins with Cornelius.

[13] So also O. Bauernfeind, *Die Apostelgeschichte* (HKNT 5: Leipzig: A. Deichert, 1939) 54; see also M. Dibelius, *Studies in the Acts of the Apostles,* trans. M. Ling (London: SCM Press, 1956) 8ff.

[14] So Haenchen, 189; cf. Bauernfeind, 54.

[15] Concerning the historical problems of this text: J. Munck, *Paul and the Salvation of Mankind,* trans. Frank Clarke (Richmond: John Knox Press, 1960), 239ff. Agreeing with Baur and Schwartz, Munck deletes *tōn pepisteukotōn.* Without doubt the text presents difficult historical problems so that Baur's question is appropriate: "We must ask, how did all these thousands of believing Jews come into a church, which, according to all accounts, could not have been very important" (quoted by Munck, 241 n. 1). We are examining Luke's viewpoint, however, and he has prepared for "the myriads" by means of his reports of mass conversions.

[16] It is obvious that the numbers are not to be understood mathmatically. They are to represent symbolically the goodwill of Jews at the reception of the preaching of the gospel.

[17] Concerning *mallon* see W. Bauer, *A Greek-English Lexicon of the New Testament,* trans. W. F. Arndt and F. W. Gingrich (Chicago: University of Chicago Press, 1957) 490.

[18] F. J. Foakes-Jackson and Kirsopp Lake eds. *The Beginnings of Christianity IV: The Acts of the Apostles,* K. Lake and H. Cadbury (London: Macmillan, 1933) 66, characterizes 6:7 as "a unique statement, and there is no other trace of any tendency of the priests to become Christians." See also Conzelmann, *Apostelgeschichte,* 44f. The priests have no significance for the structure of the community. For Luke the notice shows that the Jewish leaders as a group do not oppose the mission.

[19] Commentators know that vv. 42 and 43 fit together poorly because they are doublets, and that v. 43 breaks the connection between vv. 42 and 44. As in 5:14, Luke has interpolated a remark into an old narrative that has been handed down to him: Many Jews and proselytes became believers and were exhorted to continue in the grace of God (cf. 11:23). Once more Luke has toned down an account that emphasized a one-sided rejection by the Jews. We may assume that at the time of Luke it was customary to give such a description of Jews. The scene in Chapter 13 was thus originally intended to describe rejection of the gospel by Jews, as the pregnant use of "the Jews" in v. 45 shows. Many Jews were actually converted (so correctly Bauernfeind, 178, and Foakes-Jackson, 119).

[20] Haenchen, 193 n. 2: " 'The Jews' show no enmity to the Christians until 12:3."

[21] According to Conzelmann, Haenchen, Loisy and others, *epeithonto*

cannot mean that a portion of the Jews has been converted since the scene is designed to show that the Jews are without hope. If this is the intention, then Luke has certainly designed the scene unskillfully. For it presents a two-fold picture of Jews who are divided over the missionary preaching and it speaks of two decisions. Even if Luke does not intend to report that some have been converted, one must ask why he has allowed a division among the Jews to be so evident, provided that he wants to depict a comprehensive obduracy and rejection. We consider it probable that Luke has altered a narrative that was handed down to him. Originally the scene had been designed to show an absolute rejection on the part of the Jews. Luke, however, has toned down this understanding and maintains instead that some have nevertheless been converted by the missionary preaching. This cannot be removed from the text. Perhaps Luke has remained cautious toward a view that includes only Jewish rejection because this would raise difficulties for his understanding of the continuity of salvation history (see n. 19).

[22] Thus N. A. Dahl, 324. H. Conzelmann *(Theology,* 152) is hardly correct when he maintains that the concepts which indicate the position of Israel within salvation history are transferred to the church, which is made up of Jews and Gentiles. The concept "Israel" is never used by Luke as a term for a church made up of Jews and Gentiles. In addition, *laos* refers first to Israel, then to the church. Where *laos* refers to the church (15:14; 18:10), it is indefinite: "a large group of people" or "a people from the Gentiles" (15:14), in addition to those who, strictly speaking, make up the people, the Jews who believe in the Messiah. 18:10 is even more indefinite: God has many people in Corinth.

[23] Cf. H. von Soden, *adelphos TDNT* I, ed. G. Kittel, trans. G. Bromiley (Grand Rapids, Mich.: Wm. B. Eerdmans, 1964) 144-146.

[24] See Munck, 234f.

[25] Haenchen, 448.

[26] Dahl, 326f.

[27] *Ibid.*

[28] "The true Israel" is not meant (so Bauernfeind, 70), but simply Israel. For Luke there is only one Israel.

[29] F. Hahn, 134.

[30] Missionary preaching is already a part of proof from Scripture. See Dupont, 139.

[31] In *The Beginnings of Christianity* (IV, 9) the question is stated clearly: If the apostles knew and understood already at the beginning from the command of Jesus that the gospel was to be preached to Gentiles, why then are they shown so hesitant in Chapters 6-15?

[32] Dibelius, 109f.; Wilckens, 64f.

[33] Wilckens, *ibid*.

[34] According to Wilckens, 65, this is hardly meant to be universalistic.

[35] The grammatical difficulty of v. 36 can be understood in such a way that *ton logon* is an appositive to what precedes so that the meaning is that God does not unjustly favor but has accepted the God-fearer in every nation . . . , this is the word that he has sent to the children of Israel. See H. Mosbech, *Sproglig Fortolkning til Apostlenes Gerninger* (Copenhagen: J. H. Schultz, 1944) 103. So understood it would mean that the apostles turn from Israel to all peoples in their preaching and that this salvation is to be given to the world *via* Israel.

[36] See below, Part V.

[37] Bauernfeind, 39f.: These Jews do not represent diaspora Judaism, but the Gentiles; see also Dupont, 144, and Hahn, 173.

[38] Haenchen, 184, remarks that the audience could hardly recognize a reference to the Gentile mission, though such a reference is not thereby excluded. Nevertheless, the question here is how Luke himself has seen the matter, and accordingly it can hardly be doubted that the Gentiles are included in the picture.

[39] Whether the resurrection of Jesus or his earthly appearances is intended—most commentators argue for the latter—is irrelevant. Decisive for interpretation is 13:46, in which the Gentiles are clearly implied.

[40] Dahl, 327.

[41] So Conzelmann, *Apostelgeschichte*, 35; Bauernfeind, 70; Haenchen, 209.

[42] Most commentators: Christ; otherwise, Dupont, 146.

[43] Concerning 3:26, Bauernfeind, 70, remarks that the sources Luke follows here contain earlier ideas, according to which Jesus was sent to the Jews, while the other peoples are joined to the holy people, to the "empirical" Israel, which because of its conversion, will become the true Israel. Luke explains differently: Jesus was sent primarily to Jews and then to Gentiles. From the speeches to Jews, however, one gets the definite impression that Jesus was sent to the Jews who are to be representatives of the peoples so that the peoples are reached

through Israel (see James' speech in 15:16f.). We can say only that the conception found, according to Bauernfeind, in Luke's sources is precisely that of Luke. Luke knows only the "empirical" Israel.

[44] See the explanation of Wilckens, 52f., in which it is emphasized that the passage deals with the preaching to Jews of the diaspora. If they as representatives of all Israel fail to confess Jesus, then salvation history will in the future bypass Israel, and the gospel will be turned over to the Gentiles instead of Israel. The historical fate of the diaspora is to be understood in this way.

[45] Haenchen, 417f.; see also Conzelmann, *Apostelgeschichte,* 78.

[46] Concerning 15:14, see Dahl, "A People for His Name."

[47] See note 21.

[48] Hahn, 134f., thinks that the Lukan description of Paul's preaching does not deal primarily with the covenant and the promises to the fathers, but was determined by the providence of the creator; this is shown by 14:15 and 17:22-31. If Hahn means by this that Paul speaks differently to technically "pure" Gentiles than to Jews, this may be correct. But then it is wrong to assert that the Lukan Paul does not consider the promises of Israel and the sharing in them as decisive for Gentiles as well.

[49] Haenchen, 101.

[50] See above, Part IV.

[51] Haenchen, 630: The prerogatives of the Jewish people are annulled by a Gentile mission without circumcision. That is, historically considered, correct, but is it Lukan?

[52] Thus, Dupont, 148; concerning the question of composition and redaction in the Cornelius narrative: Conzelmann, *Apostelgeschichte,* 61f.; Dibelius, 109ff.; Bauernfeind, 141; Haenchen, 355ff.; Munck, 228ff.

[53] Dibelius, 122.

[54] So also Conzelmann, *Apostelgeschichte,* 61f.

[55] Dupont, 149, on the Cornelius episode: ". . . it constitutes the step by which Christianity crossed over the limits of Judaism." As a historical statement this may be correct, but is it Lukan? For Luke the church stands in unbroken continuity with Judaism, whereas some of the Jews have denied true Judaism. For views corresponding to Dupont's, see O'Neill, 70.

[56] Cf. *Beginnings IV,* 125.

[57] So correctly Haenchen, 101.

The Twelve on Israel's Thrones

Luke's Understanding
of the
Apostolate

I

Most investigations of Luke's view of the apostolate differ only slightly on the question of the ecclesiastical role played by the apostles. This unanimity rests upon a consensus in the understanding of the Lukan concept of the church. The first presupposition is that Luke sees the church as an independent entity—institution or organization—with emphasis on the distance from, and the break with, the synagogue and Judaism. The second presupposition is that the church is the new or true Israel, which marks both the continuity of salvation history and the break with the former people of God. The former people of God, Israel, has completed her role in history and is relieved or replaced by the church. The understanding of the twelve apostles lies within the framework sketched above.[1] The apostles are usually understood as "Institut der Kirche";[2] as the origin of ecclesiastical offices;[3] as regents or leaders of the new Israel,[4] the church; as guarantors of the Jesus tradition,[5] which in turn is the foundation of the church; or as missionaries.[6]

But if Luke does not see the church as the new Israel, these interpretations immediately become problematic. What role do the Twelve play if Luke knows only one Israel, the old Israel? It is at least clear that what may be called a common opinion, despite differences in details and emphases, conflicts with some characteristic texts in Luke-Acts. One such text is the unique farewell discourse in Luke 22:24ff, in which the Twelve are given an eschatological role as future regents over Israel. If this text is to fit in with the usual scheme, the twelve tribes of Israel must be a designation of the new people of God. But this conflicts with what Luke says elsewhere concerning Israel as the people of twelve tribes.[7] Another possibility is that the text has no meaning for Luke's conception of the apostolate, that it is a vestige or reminiscence of Jewish Christian tradition.[8] This view is also applied to another significant text, Luke 24:13ff. Here we do not have a direct reference to the Twelve. It is significant, however, that the Emmaus travellers' main problem is the question about Israel (24:21).[9] In light of Jesus' interpretation of Scripture in which he is the one to redeem Israel and in light of Luke 22:29f. it is unsatisfactory to speak about Jewish Christian reminiscences.[10]

The problem is further complicated by the disciples' question in Acts 1:6. The resurrection and the outpouring of the Spirit are interpreted as heralding the restoration of Israel. Again we can simply call it a Jewish Christian vestige, even understood psychologically; the Twelve have not overcome their Jewish past [11]—in spite of Jesus' tutoring (1:3f.). But this is hardly satisfactory. And it is amazing that precisely these men are viewed as guarantors for the *historia Jesu*. Finally we have Acts 1:15-26 on the election of a new apostle.[12] Later we shall discuss why it is necessary to elect a new twelfth apostle. In the context the number twelve has a decisive function, but commentators have been unable to give a satisfactory explanation for the importance it has for Luke.[13] They often see a contrast between this statement and the theology of

Luke as a whole and therefore assign it to pre-Lukan tradition.[14] But this is difficult in light of the texts discussed above —the statements connecting Israel and the Twelve, which are concentrated in the conclusion of Luke's Gospel and the beginning of Acts. It is obvious that the picture of "the new Israel" does not fit with any of these texts. Scholars have unanimously agreed, as seen by their description of such texts as pre-Lukan Jewish Christian remnants.

If, on the other hand, we can see that Luke neither uses nor is acquainted with the concept of the church as the new or true Israel, a new interpretation is possible. It becomes clear that Luke's conception of the twelve apostles is shaped by his theology of Israel, and that the Twelve are essential to his understanding of Israel and its fate. This in turn determines his ecclesiology.

II

An examination of the placement of sayings about the Twelve indicates their significance for Luke. As is well-known, the apostles play no role in the latter half of Acts. They are referred to for the last time in connection with the Apostolic Council (15:2, 4, 6, 22f.; 16:4).[15] Closer observation shows that their role shifts after Chapter 7. Stephen's sermon, which marks the conclusion of missionary activity in Jerusalem, signifies the end of the apostles' direct missionary activity to Israel. After Chapter 7 they are mentioned on three important occasions. First, the initial reference to "the nations," to the peoples outside Israel (Chaps. 10-11) is related to Peter, who throughout Luke-Acts is reckoned as one of the Twelve. As we have demonstrated elsewhere, this reference to "the nations" is a part of God's promise to Israel.[16] In other words, even the mission initiated among the Gentiles is related positively to Israel. Apart from Chaps. 10-11 Acts records no missionary activity among the Gentiles by Peter or the Twelve.

Second, Acts 8:14ff. connects the Twelve with Samaria. This is not a Gentile mission, since for Luke the Samaritans are not considered Gentiles, but "the lost sheep of the house of Israel." [17] The Samaritans receive the Spirit, which Luke sees as Israel's "possession" (8:15ff.). Third, the Twelve legitimize Paul (9:26ff.). Paul is seen in Acts as a diaspora missionary and teacher of Israel! Just as the first proclamation to the Gentiles concerned Israel, so also the conversion of the Samaritans and the legitimation of Paul relate to Israel. Since the real problem in Acts 15 is the relationship of the nations to the law of Moses,[18] the composition indicates that the apostles disappear from the narrative at this point because their mission to Israel is accomplished.

In contrast to Matthew and Mark, Luke has given the Twelve a greater place in the life of Jesus.[19] In a number of instances Luke simply follows Mark [6:13; 9; (1, 10) 12; (18:31); 22:3(14ff.)47]; but in contrast to Mark (and Matthew) he underscores repeatedly the concept "apostle." At the same time, Luke has special references to the apostles (8:1; 11:49; 17:5). In general, the apostles play a notably passive role during Jesus' earthly life. Apart from the mission in 9:1ff., the apostles participate mainly as observers of the events, as do the other disciples and even the entire Jewish population. As is commonly recognized, Luke does not envelope the life of Jesus in secrecy. Everything happens in public, while all Israel watches,[20] which in turn is a presupposition in Acts for the preaching of repentance to Israel.[21] There seems to be little conscious effort in the way Luke introduces his comments on the twelve apostles. Even the public nature of Jesus' ministry in Luke runs contrary to the view that the task of the Twelve is to be eye-witnesses to guarantee the Jesus-tradition—a task that can be fulfilled by the wider circle of disciples as well as by the Jewish nation as a whole. As a result, sayings about the life of Jesus are seldom found on the lips of the apostles in Acts.

Only on two occasions in the Gospel do the Twelve play a more determinative role. The first occurs in the passion story, more precisely in the account of the Lord's Supper (22:14ff.). What is more important is that this is the part of the passion story Luke has most thoroughly reworked, i.e., the discourse in 22:24-37. Several observations reveal the importance of the discourse. This is the last speech of Jesus during his earthly life. The material derives partly from Mark (10:41ff.), partly from Q (Luke 22:30=Matt. 19:28;[22]), and finally from Luke's special material, (22:28-29). As a composition, the discourse is undoubtedly Luke's work. Furthermore, this is Jesus' farewell discourse.[23] It has the style of the farewell discourse with its retrospective view, admonitions, decrees, and future perspective. Verses 28ff. are clearly Jesus' last will and testament.[24] In this discourse the future role of the Twelve [25] is decisive since they will exercise ruling authority just as Jesus has. Above all, the Twelve are specially related to Israel (v. 30).[26] They are not presented as ecclesiastical regents, but as Israel's eschatological rulers and judges. The very location of this passage in the composition makes it unlikely that in this important discourse Luke is simply handing on Jewish Christian reminiscences without their having any meaning for him.[27]

Luke has shown great concern for the events occurring between Jesus' death and the outpouring of the Spirit (Luke 24 and Acts 1). In this section we find the most important statements about the Twelve, besides those in the farewell discourse in Luke 22. In other words, the Twelve are especially associated with the resurrection, as could have been expected in light of the definitive statement in Acts 1:21. According to Mark 16:7, the announcement of the discovery of the empty tomb was to be given to "his disciples and Peter"; Matt. 28:8 declares that the message was given to "his disciples." Luke, on the other hand, stresses that the women told "the eleven and all the rest" (24:9). The following verse even adds: the women gave the message to the "apostles" (24:10).

The story of the journey to Emmaus, especially 24:33, also betrays Luke's concern to emphasize the apostles or the Twelve, precisely where such an emphasis is awkward. The travellers to Emmaus are to take to "the eleven and those who were together with them" the news that their doubt about Jesus as Israel's redeemer has been dispelled (cf. 24:21, 25ff.). However, once among the apostles they find that the apostles already believe: "The Lord has risen indeed, and has appeared to Simon!" (24:34). Without referring to a particular appearance to Peter, Luke portrays the leader of the apostles as the first to have received a christophany. In passing we shall only mention that for Luke the discovery of the empty tomb does not function as a proof (24:11, 24).[28]

The speech in 24:36-49, which may also be characterized as a farewell discourse, though it is not as formal as 22:14 ff., does not specifically identify its addressees. But in light of 24:9f, 33f, there is little doubt that it was primarily directed to the Eleven. This is confirmed in Acts 1:2f, in which it is mentioned that Jesus "gave commandment" to his apostles after the resurrection; *enteilamenos* can only refer back to the speech, 24:44ff, or possibly also to 22:14ff, where once again only the Twelve are present. Acts 1:3 makes it clear that it is to the Twelve Jesus reveals himself after his resurrection (cf. also 13:31,[29] 10:41). Furthermore, in the speech in 24:36ff, esp. vv. 44 and 46, Jesus points back to what he had said earlier, namely, to the passion predictions. Only the third passion prediction is referred to here because of the references to Scripture. Such a reference is found only in Luke 18:31ff., where Jesus promises the fulfillment of everything written of the Son of Man by the prophets. Only the Eleven would understand the statements in 24:44, 46. The reference to the Twelve in Luke 18:31ff. has been taken over from Mark 10:32. But with the decisive reference to the Scripture in Chapter 24 the Twelve are once again set apart. They are set apart wherever the resurrection, the Messiah of Israel, or the redemption of God's people are discussed. Luke's references to the Twelve are arranged and constructed to indicate a special relationship between the resurrection of Jesus and subsequent events, and the Twelve. We shall return to the idea that the resurrection in Luke is specifically a Jewish concern.

What is expressed in Luke 24 by comments on traditional material is found *expressis verbis* in Acts 1. This opening chapter in Acts is devoted entirely to Jesus' last meeting with the eleven apostles and to the story of the election of a new twelfth apostle. The latter half of the chapter is a coherent story (vv. 15-26). The first section consists partly of historical information and comment, which also serve to interpret what Luke has said in his Gospel (vv. 2-4, 12-14), and partly of a dialogue between Jesus and the Eleven with a promise of the Spirit [30] and missionary instruction (6-8), to which is added a short account of the ascension (9-11).

The importance of this section (vv. 1-14) for understanding Acts as a whole cannot be overestimated. The very location of the paragraph as a prelude to Acts is significant. The theme of Acts and of the coming events is introduced (1:4f. 8, 11). But at the same time the passage is retrospective. Acts 1:2 points back to the election of the Twelve, with another list in 1:13. We are also told what happened in the period following Jesus' resurrection (1:3); Jesus spent forty days teaching the Eleven about the kingdom of God.[31] Luke relates the preaching of the Eleven directly to Jesus' preaching and the line is also drawn directly back to the farewell discourse (22:14ff.), especially to the saying that the Twelve shall be entrusted with *basileia,* in the same way Jesus received it (22:29).[32] There can be no doubt that this *basileia* (22:29) is linked to the restoration of Israel, that it is "the kingdom for Israel" (22:29f). In this context 24:21 also belongs which speaks of Jesus as the one to redeem Israel.

The manner in which Luke connects messiahship with the kingdom of God is clearly described in Luke 1-2 as well as in the speeches in the first part of Acts. At the same time, Acts 1:3 prepares us for the question in 1:6. The doubt of those on the road to Emmaus and the triumph over this doubt also reveal the relationship between messiahship and the kingdom of God (Luke 24:21ff.). Jesus' reference to his messiahship according to the Scriptures (24:44ff.) determines the form of the question in Acts 1:6. There is no longer any doubt that the kingdom will be restored to Israel.[33] The Eleven are now certain of this in light of the resurrection. The only question is *when* this restoration will take place. Within the framework of Acts, reference is made to such a restoration, primarily in Acts 15:16ff.[34] Therefore the connection between the Twelve and Israel is stressed (Acts 1).

Finally we come to the election of the twelfth apostle (Acts 1:15-26)—an election taking place according to Scripture (1:20), and decided by God himself.[35] Although not a single word in the passage indicates that the election has anything specifically to do with Luke's understanding of Israel, the connection between the two is suggested by Luke 22 and 24 and the rest of Acts 1. At least two things are clear. First, the task of the Twelve is to bear witness to the resurrection of Jesus (1:22).[36] Secondly, there must be twelve apostles, at least during a certain period of history. After the death of James (Acts 12:2) it would be not only unnecessary, but superfluous, to elect a new apostle, for reasons which Luke makes clear. If a new apostle were elected, the eschatological Israel would have thirteen regents over the twelve tribes!

III

Why is it ncessary for Luke to inform us about the election of a twelfth apostle? The point is not only that a twelfth apostle is chosen. Luke stresses the election in a formal way, describing it as the fulfillment of Scripture and as an election[37] by God himself with the result that the importance of what happens receives still greater emphasis.

Commentaries and monographs share a widespread uncertainty about the meaning of Acts 1:15-26.[38] Reference is occasionally made without further explanation to "the sacred number twelve";[39] elsewhere it is said that the apostolic circle must have the same *modus* in the church as it had during the life of Jesus [40]—in which case it becomes somewhat difficult to understand why no mention is made of a new election after the death of James (Acts 12:2). Only rarely is the election linked to Luke's understanding of Israel and its relationship to the message of Jesus. The reason is that Acts 1:15ff. is usually viewed as a piece of traditional material which clashes with the rest of Luke's presentation in Acts. But whether from a linguistic, stylistic or theological perspective it is difficult to see that Acts 1:15ff. is not Lukan. Even if Luke is using traditional material, he had given it such a prominent position in Acts that he must have had a special reason for including it.

There is no doubt that the link between the number twelve and the apostolic circle is traditional. It is sufficient to point to Mark and the way in which Luke uses him. A concordance shows that Mark refers more often than Luke to the Twelve. The question is only whether Luke ever reveals that the precise number twelve as applied to the apostolic circle is essential for him,[41] and that this circle can only function with the correct number. About this there should be no doubt, since it is substantiated by a number of references.

In the account of Judas' betrayal, Luke is not satisfied with Mark 14:10 and Matthew 26:14, which describe Judas as "one of the twelve." He uses rather the more elaborate description of Judas: "of the number of the twelve" (Luke 22:3).

Whatever else this means, it implies that the number twelve is essential. Whereas Mark and Matthew in this context accentuate Judas' membership in the chosen circle, Luke shifts the accent slightly. Judas belongs to a group for which the number twelve is constitutive. Acts 1:17 shows that the formulation in Luke 22:3 is not merely incidental. It is unclear how v. 17 functions syntactically in its context. However, the essential point is how Luke understands Judas' membership in the apostolic circle: "For he was numbered among us, and was allotted his share in this ministry." In the two parallel clauses the numerical significance of the twelve and the "office" are stressed. By itself *katarithmeō* need mean nothing more than "to belong." However, it seems unlikely that it would mean only this. In the first place, since Luke indisputably emphasizes the number twelve in Luke 22:3, the close relationship of Acts 1:17 to Luke 22:3 indicates a similar emphasis in Acts 1:17.

In the second place, *arithmeō and katarithmeō* occur only in these two places in Luke-Acts. When Luke wishes to express membership he uses other words. If the *hoti* clause in Acts 1:17 serves as a direct support for election of a new apostle, then the basis for the new election must lie in the number twelve itself. But even if the syntax is not to be understood in this way, it is obvious that the number twelve plays an important role. The new election is necessary to complete this number. This is also underscored by the statement regarding Matthias' position after the election; "he was enrolled *(sygkatepsēphisthē)* with the eleven apostles" (Acts 1:26). This verb which is infrequent in classical Greek also has numerical significance for Luke. This is indicated by the parallels with

Luke 22:3 and Acts 1:17. In addition the only variant of the verb found in the New Testament occurs in Acts 19:19 where the numerical significance is indisputable.

These three passages are conclusive evidence that it is the very number twelve that is constitutive, and that the function of the apostolic circle can only be carried out by twelve.

However, we have not yet determined why the number twelve is important for Luke. But about this there should be little doubt. The notion that the apostolic circle must have the same *modus* as it had during Jesus' life [42] provides no explanation for the number itself. Luke does not even hint at such an idea anywhere in his work.

On the contrary, the circle of the Twelve is linked explicitly to the concept "Israel," primarily as it is seen in the eucharistic discourse (Luke 22:30).[43] Here the task of the apostles is to be regents and judges over the twelve tribes of Israel.[44] It is easy to explain why Luke's statement at this point differs from Matthew 19:28,[45] lacking the number twelve with regard to the thrones. In 19:28, Matthew has obviously failed to give careful consideration to the figure of Judas; in the context Jesus is speaking to his "disciples" (19:23, 25), not to the apostles or the Twelve. Naturally for Matthew the Twelve are also "disciples," explaining why in certain situations they are called "the twelve disciples" (10:1; 11:1). Usually they are designated simply as "the twelve" (10:5; 20:17; 26:14, 20). But Matthew does not identify "the disciples" with the Twelve.

Matthew places no emphasis on the number twelve itself in the paranetic material in 19:16ff. It is not the apostolate as such, but the paranesis that is determinative. Luke 22 is significantly different. Because Judas is present for the farewell discourse, Luke cannot permit Jesus to give the Twelve the promise of being judges over Israel; one of them will be left out.[46] Consequently he speaks only about "thrones." This omission indicates that Luke has reflected upon the statement, and not merely allowed it to slip through as tradition.

Another passage illustrates the importance of the link between the Twelve and Israel for Luke. In his defense before Agrippa, Paul claims that the fulfillment of the promise of the resurrection is the focal point of Israel's worship (Acts 26:6f.). In this connection Luke employs the concept *dōdeka-phylon;* Israel is the people of twelve tribes. It makes no difference whether Luke is thinking about the messianic restoration of the twelve tribes, or to the contemporary Israel as a people of twelve tribes. It is important that the number twelve in connection with the twelve tribes is associated with his conception of Israel. Obviously, Luke is not describing the church as the new Israel, even if understood along the lines of James 1:1 (cf. 1 Pet. 1:1). The passage also touches upon the hope of the resurrection as the main feature of Jewish expectation. The restoration of Israel is the same as the hope of resurrection. Other statements in Luke referring to the cult of Israel, esp. Luke 1-2, show that the hope of Israel's deliverance and restoration is central. The unceasing worship night and day is exemplified (Luke 2:37) by the prophetess Anna, who is waiting for "the deliverance of Israel" (2:38).

Acts 26:5f. furthers our understanding of the significance of the Twelve for Luke. Here he links Israel—*basileia*—resurrection—messiahship. Before dealing with this in detail, however, we must consider one more feature in his portrait of the Twelve.

Luke makes an effort to show that the stance and status of the Twelve derive directly from God himself and are in agreement with Scripture.[47] Jesus is not the sole founder of the apostolate. Naturally, Luke knows from his tradition that Jesus chose the Twelve, and this he does not deny. Nevertheless, part of his task is to show that the choice is also divine.

This thought is expressed first in Luke 6:12ff., in the reworking of Mark 3:13-19.[48] The Markan text is altered in two ways. While Mark incorporates the passage completely into a narrative context with only the aid of a simple paratactic construction *(kai anabainei* . . .), Luke uses a formal introductory formula that he elsewhere uses for accentuation: *egeneto de en tais hēmerais tautais* (6:12 cf. 1:5; 2:1 (3:1); (5:17); 9:51 (17:11) [49] Furthermore, to Mark's statement that Jesus went up onto the mountain (Mark 3:13), Luke adds that Jesus spent the night praying to God. The comparison with Mark's text shows that Luke wants to stress that the choosing of the Twelve is divinely sanctioned.[50] At the same time Luke has omitted the reason Mark gives for choosing the Twelve, namely, that they are to be with Jesus and are to be sent out to preach (3:14). According to Luke the Twelve are chosen neither to follow Jesus nor to be sent out as preachers during Jesus' activity on earth. Their primary task lies in the future.

Further evidence of the divine choosing of the apostolate is Luke 11:49. The wording of the quotation from Q introduced by Luke (cf. Matt. 23:34) has clearly been altered. It is impossible to determine the original wording of the saying. It is equally impossible to say whether Luke intends it to be understood as a quotation from Scripture or as a direct pronouncement from God, reading *sophia tou theou* as a circumlocution for God.[51] In any case, it is significant that the sending out of the apostles to Israel (Luke 11:47-54 is a speech addressed to the scribes and the Pharisees!) refers back to a direct pronouncement by God. The juxtaposition of prophets and apostles ought not to be overlooked, since in Acts the Twelve are portrayed more as prophets than as missionaries. The application of the concept "missionary" to the Twelve fits poorly with Luke's ecclesiology.

The third time that the choosing of the apostles is mentioned is Acts 1:2. Here it is said that Jesus chose the Twelve *(exelexato).* But it is also said that it is "through the Holy

Spirit." Syntactically, the phrase does not belong with *enteil-amenos,* which would be meaningless. It is emphasized that the choosing of the apostles took place through the Spirit, thus relating it back to God. We might note in passing that the Spirit according to Luke is a characteristic feature of Israel, "a possession" of the people of God.

Further support is found in Acts 1:15-26.[52] What is stressed first of all is the association between Scripture and the apostolate. Judas' fate is in itself a fulfillment of Scripture (1:16b-20a).[53] Furthermore, the election of a new apostle is warranted by a direct reference to Scripture (1:20b-21). God has given instruction in Scripture that a new apostle shall be appointed in Judas' place. On the basis of the quotation from Psa. 109:8 in Acts 1:20b, the conclusion is drawn "so one of the men who have accompanied us . . . must become . . ." [54] The justification is given neither by reference to a *modus* the apostolic circle had during Jesus' life nor by reference to Jesus as the one who chooses. The new apostle is selected by God. This is evident from the prayer that accompanies the election. The appeal we find here, "Lord who knowest the hearts of all men . . . ," can only refer to God himself according to Lukan usage (see Acts 15:8).[55] The casting of lots simply reveals the one whom God had already chosen to replace Judas.

Peter's speech in Acts 10:36ff. provides final confirmation of this viewpoint. According to v. 41 the Twelve—in the context the reference can apply to no one else [56]—have been chosen in advance by God (*prokecheirotonēmenois hypo tou theou*).[57] How much weight should be given to the prefix *pro* is uncertain. But at any rate it can be interpreted to mean that the choosing of the Twelve goes back further than Jesus. Luke 11:49 shows that by choosing the Twelve Jesus fulfills the will of God. It ought to be a simple matter to find the reason why Luke is not satisfied with pointing to Jesus' choosing of the Twelve as final authority. Luke presents neither Jesus' messiahship nor his resurrection as unquestioned axioms. Luke takes great pains to show, prove, and demonstrate Jesus' messiahship and his resurrection.[58] It is precisely of this that the apostles are witnesses. Consequently, it must be shown that their authority goes back further than Jesus, namely, to God himself.

IV

The number twelve is significant for Luke in so far as the twelve apostles are appointed over Israel. According to Luke 22:30 the Twelve will serve as regents in the eschatological Israel.[59] In the account in Acts 1:21 the task of the Twelve consists of bearing witness to Jesus' resurrection. Any direct connection between the two statements is not immediately apparent. Therefore, commentators have said that the eschatological function of the Twelve according to Luke 22 disappears in Acts because of the historicizing tendency,[60] or that it continues to live on only as a weak traditional reminiscense.[61]

The link between the two statements, however, becomes clearer when we observe how Luke deals with concepts such as *basileia* and Jesus' messiahship.[62] As we have already indicated above, resurrection faith is a real concern for Israel, a characteristic of the cult of the people of God. This is most obvious in Acts 26:6ff. in which the worship of the people of the twelve tribes is directed toward the coming resurrection. The resurrection in this context is characterized as "God's promise to the fathers" (26:6) and thus can be described simply as "Israel's hope" (26:6-7). Furthermore, the resurrection (Act 26:5) is characterized as specifically Pharisaic. This view is again underscored by the scene before the Sanhedrin (Acts 23, see especially v. 6-8), in which the resurrection is the very hope of Israel (v. 6). Similarily in the discussion with the Roman Jews (28:20) Paul says that it is because of Israel's hope that he has been imprisoned.

The same point is emphasized by reference to Moses and the prophets in Acts 26:22-23. Luke stresses that the resurrection is the fulfillment of Scripture. He alone of the synoptic writers takes up this motif in the conclusion of the Gospel (24:25-27, 32, 44-46). Luke does not refer to the passion predictions as sayings of Jesus in such a way that the resurrection is seen as the fulfillment of Jesus' predictions. On the contrary, they are understood in such a way that during his life Jesus expressed what the Scripture said about the passion and resurrection of the Messiah (cf. 18:31ff. compared with 24:44ff.).[63] In his Gospel Luke is content with general references to Moses and the prophets and not with direct quotations from Scripture, whereas in Acts detailed exegesis of this point is found (2:25ff. 13:32ff.). We mention at this point only that both of these passages link the concept of the messianic *basileia* to the resurrection texts (see 2:30; 13:33f.). References to Scripture are important because for Luke the Scripture is the holy book of the people of God, just as the law for him is Israel's identifying feature. Characteristic of the apostolic preaching, including Paul's, is its basis in interpretation of Scripture (cf. 2:17ff., 25ff.; 3:22ff.; 13:33ff.). Jesus is not called upon as the final authority, for he is the one who is to be "verified."

The resurrection is therefore characterized as Israel's specific concern, God's promise to his people. Since the primary task of the Twelve according to Acts 1:22 is to witness to the resurrection, the connection with the farewell discourse in Luke 22:30 concerning the twelve regents over the twelve tribes of Israel is clear.[64] For this reason we must look more closely at the idea of *basileia* in the farewell discourse (22:29). Luke links the idea of *basileia* to the circle of the Twelve, as has already been noted in connection with Acts 1:2, 6. If we understand this last reference not as a Jewish remnant in Lukan tradition, but as an expression of Luke's own intentions, then the meaning is that the *basileia* Jesus proclaims is precisely the "kingdom" Israel waits for, that which has been promised to the people of God. Luke 1-2 [65] makes this clear, especially Luke 1:32, 33: God will give Jesus the throne of his father David; he will reign over the house of Jacob forever; his *basileia* will be without end.[66] The agreement with Acts 2:30 is obvious. God had sworn to set "one of David's descendents upon his throne."

This enthronement is related to the resurrection by means of Psa. 16:8ff. whose interpretation is based on the fact that David died and was buried and that "his tomb is with us to this day" (2:29-32). Within this understanding of the resurrection as enthronement the Twelve are included as witnesses (2:32b). David himself had spoken of the resurrection of the Messiah as fulfilling the promise to Israel (2:31). The Twelve may now proclaim Jesus as Lord and Christ before the "whole house of Israel" (2:36). Naturally, this means the Messiah of Israel, since Luke knows no other. The testimony of the Twelve is that God has fulfilled his promise to his people. Not only is the scriptural testimony important, but David himself testified about the one who will sit on his throne.[67] The Spirit also testifies that Israel's Messiah has come (2:33ff.).

We have referred only to one passage within Luke 1-2. However, the entire section is permeated with the same thought: the inauguration of this phase of history beginning with Jesus is nothing but the fulfillment of God's promise to the fathers (1:16-17, 32-33, 51-54, 68-79; 2:10-11, 25, 29-32, 38). This theme is also found in the speeches in Acts. We have already considered the speech in Chapter 2. The speech in Acts 3:11ff. stresses that it is "the God of Abraham, and of Isaac and of Jacob, the God of our fathers" who raised Jesus from the dead (3:13, 15); the passion and the resurrection reveal Jesus as Israel's Messiah and as the prophet spoken of by Moses (3:18-22); the Messiah's parousia means the re-establishment spoken of by the prophets (3:21).[68] In Acts 5:30 Luke maintains once again that it is "the God of our fathers" who has raised Jesus; his resurrection/exaltation occurred in order to give Israel repentance and forgiveness of sins (5:31).

The Spirit also bears witness to "these things" (5:32b). The testimony of the apostles and of the Spirit is that Israel has received salvation, repentance and forgiveness of sins; they do not witness to the resurrection *per se*. Furthermore, in 10:42, the consequence of the resurrection is that for Israel Jesus is proclaimed as the established judge of the living and the dead. The same views are found in Paul's speech in Pisidian Antioch (13:16-41). The speech begins with a historical survey, or a "historical creed" [69] for Israel, that emphasizes the election of the fathers by "the God of this people, Israel" (v. 17). Jesus is the son of David whom God gave to Israel as Savior according to the promise to David (v. 23). This promise to David and the promise to the fathers are fulfilled for the people by the resurrection of Jesus (vv. 32ff.). The apostles' testimony to Jesus' resurrection is simply the proclamation of the fulfillment of the promise to Israel (vv. 31ff.). Therefore, the Twelve are also characterized as Jesus' witnesses before the people (10:42). [70]

The Old Testament texts that are cited are further proof that the resurrection of Jesus implies the salvation and restoration of Israel, the fulfillment of God's promise to his people. And it is in this context that the apostles appear as witnesses to the resurrection of Jesus. The main point of the witness is not simply that the resurrection has occurred, but that Jesus is the Messiah God has promised his people, and that Israel's restoration has now begun.

The last time the apostles appear in Acts is at the Apostolic Council (15:2, 6, 22). The reason Luke allows them to fade from the picture at this point is that their earthly task is now finished as James' speech explains (15:13-21). [71] James says that Israel's restoration is already a fact (15:16-18). The relationship between vv. 16 and 17 can be understood only as describing the relationship between Israel and the Gentiles. Luke has described the restoration of Israel in his account of the Jewish mass conversions and the establishment of the Christian congregation in Jerusalem. That portion of Israel that has accepted Israel's Messiah and keeps the law of Moses has now emerged. For Luke the church's existence is proof that God has kept his promises to his people.

In Acts, the Twelve function as missionaries to the Jews.[72] But the term "missionary" is not sufficient and may obscure their role.[73] According to Luke, the Twelve are called to proclaim before Israel that the turning point in the history of the people of God has occurred and thereby to call the people to repentance for putting the Messiah to death. It would be more appropriate to say that Luke assigns them a prophetic role. Scene after scene in the first part of Acts shows that the Twelve address Israel with the message of God's fulfillment of the promise to his people (2:22f., 36, 39; 3:13ff., 19ff., 24ff.; 4:10ff.; 4:27; 5:30ff.) [74] And the mass conversions indicate that this message is received. The first contact with Gentiles does not represent a break with the preaching to the Jews, as I have pointed out elsewhere.[75] It is part of the promises that "a people of Gentiles" [76] should join with Israel (Acts 15:14), and furthermore that this is to be initiated by the apostles. The mission among Gentiles is not a break with Israel, but an affirmation of Israel.[77] The guarantee for this is precisely the Twelve who are chosen to play a role within Israel, since the eschatological Israel is the people of twelve tribes who are to be joined by the Gentiles.

Luke is well aware that not all the people will be converted, and furthermore that it is impossible to speak of any salvation for all Israel (cf. 3:23). The office of the Twelve as regents and judges is further illuminated by the recognized division Luke makes between the people of Israel and their leaders. While the leaders reject the proclamation of the Messiah, large segments of the people accept it. This is already clear in the Gospel, but is accentuated in Acts. In one scene after another the Jewish leaders are portrayed as obdurate. This division clearly illustrates Luke's perspective. Israel as a people is not rejected along with her leaders, which would be intolerable and unthinkable for Luke. The leaders of the people have relinquished any right to rule over the people, and the Twelve have now become the new leaders of Israel, as Luke 22:30 makes clear. Therefore, in Acts they are presented both as leaders and as those who proclaim the fulfillment of the promise to the people. They rule not over a special synagogue or a sect, a new organization or congregation, but simply over Israel. The history of the people continues in the church. As Jesus addressed the people as a whole and made demands on them, so do the Twelve.

Luke's concern for the Twelve is not for an office in the sense that such a college of twelve will always be found within the church to guide it. The Twelve are not the first ecclesiastical officials. The picture of a continuing college of twelve is not Lukan, as is clear from the eschatological emphasis of Luke 22:30 in which it is precisely these chosen ones who will rule over Israel in the last times. Further evidence is seen in the election of a new apostle, which is necessary only in one case, namely after Judas' death, but not after the death of James (1:15ff. 12:2). However morally indignant Luke must have been at Judas' action, this is not the reason that he is excluded from the Twelve. Luke says nothing definite about the time of Judas' death (Acts 1:18), but it is clear that he does not qualify for membership in the Twelve. He was not present during the forty days and thus cannot witness to the significance of the resurrection of Jesus. God's judgment of him in Scripture (Acts 1:16ff.) eliminates him as a regent over the eschatological Israel. He can render neither the eschatological nor the earthly service, which first begins after the resurrection of Jesus (Acts 1:8, 21ff.). It is different with James. A new apostle is not needed. At this time the earthly assignment of the Twelve is completed, and James has not done anything to disqualify himself from membership in the Twelve as eschatological regents.

Luke's unique ecclesiology,[78] the understanding of the church as the restored Israel, illumines another peculiarity in Acts. It is usually claimed that the Twelve are the origin of ecclesiastical offices.[79] It is not clear how this can be understood more precisely. If it is to be understood, for example, that the Twelve institute the offices, transfer authority and install office-holders, then it is mistaken. Luke has little interest in ecclesiastical institutions.[80] For him the church is the continuation of Israel's history.[81] As is well known, it is impossible to describe what kind of church order Luke conceived—episcopal, presbyterian, oligarchic, or democratic. It is just as impossible to describe how the offices and structures arise and function, as E. Schweizer has recently shown.[82]

It should be clear that for Luke the Twelve or the apostolate is not the origin of ecclesiastical offices, nor can the Twelve's position be characterized as "office." The seven "deacons" (Acts 6:1-7) do not comprise an office or permanent institution in the congregation.[83] In addition, they were elected by the congregation, not by the Twelve (6:3, 5f.).[84] It is obvious that for Luke the Seven are also a singular phenomenon. The role of the Twelve in this situation is simply to suggest a solution for the conflict and then to pray for and lay their hands upon those who are chosen (6:6).

The "elders" are also referred to in Acts. Luke's repeated reference to Jewish elders shows that this designation is not peculiarly ecclesiastical (Acts 4:5, 8, 23; 6:12; 23:14; 24:1; 25:15). The initial reference to the elders appears without any preparation and is not integrated into the account (11:30). On a few occasions they are mentioned along side the apostles or simply as authorities in the congregation (15:4, 6, 22f.; 16:4; 20:17; 21:18). It is never stated that the apostles are responsible for the establishment of such an institution. In the only reference to the election and installation of elders (Acts 14:23), Barnabas and Paul do the appointing. It is possible that Luke did not know how this institution arose. In any case, he has made no attempt to link the elders to the apostles.

The "prophets" form another group (11:27; 13:1; 15:32; 21:10). Once again, no attempt is made to link them to the Twelve or to legitimize them by appeal to the apostolate. The Spirit is poured out over the restored Israel (Acts 2:17ff.), and thus there are prophets. One reference is made to "teachers" (13:1), but just as with the other groups, no line is drawn back to the Twelve.

In other words, there is no basis for claiming that Luke traces the ecclesiastical offices back to the Twelve. The reason is that Luke's ecclesiology, coupled with his view of history, has no room for *ekklēsia* as a specific religious institution.

V

The last problem to be discussed is how the Twelve's connection with Jesus' life is to be understood. There is no question that Luke has connected the Twelve with Jesus' life differently than have the other evangelists. It is generally accepted that the Twelve function as guarantors of the ecclesiastical tradition, i.e., of the normative Jesus tradition that they can confirm in detail.[85]

This interpretation is unacceptable. Acts 1:21 clearly states that the Twelve will bear witness to Jesus' resurrection. Acts 1:21 also mentions that the new apostle must have traveled with the Eleven during the entire public ministry of Jesus, but does not indicate what significance this has. A look at the speeches in Acts casts doubt on the view that the primary task of the Twelve is to guarantee the Jesus tradition. The speeches in Acts seldom allude to the life of Jesus apart from the murder of the Messiah (2:23, 36; 3:14, 4:10; 27f.; 5:28 etc.).[86]

The first time we find a reference to the historical Jesus is Acts 2:22. The miraculous deeds of Jesus are cited as proof of God's election of him. Meanwhile, it is expressly stated that the listeners—who are Jews (2:5, 14, 22)—are themselves acquainted with what has happened: "as you yourselves know." This is in full agreement with the public character of Jesus' entire ministry according to Luke. The Emmaus travellers attest that Jesus was a prophet, "mighty in word and deed" before God and all the people (Luke 24:19) i.e., his power was demonstrated before Israel. The one thing that the listeners to the Pentecost speech do not know is what follows next in the text: Jesus' resurrection (2:24ff., 32). It may be well to note that the Western text makes an alteration in v. 22b: *eis hēmas* instead of *hymas*. This alters the meaning so that it becomes the apostles who know about the miracles and become witnesses.

The speeches in Chapters 3 and 4 make no mention of Jesus' earthly life apart from the usual statement about his death (3:15; 4:10). On the other hand, it is emphasized that the apostles have witnessed Jesus' resurrection (3:15) and that the resurrection is the essential content of their proclamation. 5:32 is somewhat indefinite, stating that the apostles are witnesses to "these things." At any rate, their witness does not concern Jesus' earthly life, but has to do with resurrection/exaltation, repentance and forgiveness of sins for Israel.

In this connection one detail in Acts 1:21f. must be defined more precisely. It is not entirely accurate to say that the qualifications for the new apostle require that he has been together with the Eleven during the whole of Jesus' earthly life and public ministry. The limits, as set down in 1:22a, are between the baptism of John and the ascension of Jesus, not his resurrection. The testimony of the Twelve that the resurrection means salvation for Israel and the fulfillment of promises, repentance and forgiveness of sins for the people of God is based on what has happened between the resurrection and the ascension. The Twelve know not only Jesus' life, but the Messiah's sayings and proclamation of the kingdom. It is also stressed in Acts 4:20 that the apostles are witnesses not simply to one event; "what we have seen and heard" includes the resurrection, Jesus' messiahship and salvation as offered to Israel (4:10, 11, 12).[87]

Among the speeches in Acts, the fullest reference to the life of Jesus occurs in 10:38f., in which special emphasis is accorded the healing miracles. In this context the apostles are also directly associated with Jesus' life as witnesses (v. 39); they know everything that Jesus did "in the country of the Jews and in Jerusalem." This speech also mentions, however, that the listeners are also aware of all that Jesus has said and done (vv. 36-38). This must simply mean that the entire life of Jesus is so widely known that it is not necessary for the Twelve to be guarantors of these events; this is true even among the Gentiles. The emphasis is not on the Jesus tradition itself, but on its significance for Israel. It is further emphasized that the apostles know this because of the resurrection and the instruction of the Risen One. It is to the Twelve that Jesus opened the Scriptures, and to them that he preached after his resurrection (Luke 24:45; Acts 1:3).

The apostles' role as witnesses has to do not with Jesus' earthly life, but with his resurrection. Here Luke states that the commission given them by the Risen One was to preach to Israel and to bear witness (*diamartyrasthai*) that Jesus is established as judge by God (10:42). On the basis of what happened after the resurrection the apostles can carry out their commission to bear witness to that which Israel neither knows nor believes. When 10:43 refers to all the prophets who bear witness (*martyrousin*) to the forgiveness of sins through Jesus, the context becomes clear. The apostles know the Scriptures and the message of the Risen One. They know the content of the resurrection.

These views are confirmed by Paul's speech in Acts 13:16ff. This speech relates little about Jesus' earthly life. It mentions Jesus' death at the hands of the Jews, makes brief reference to his role as Israel's Savior (v. 23), and notes that he followed John the Baptist (v. 24f.). Although this speech is not made by one of the Twelve, Paul invokes the witness of the Twelve— but only in connection with the resurrection (v. 31ff.).[88] The speech mentions that Jesus appeared to the Twelve after the resurrection and that they went up with him from Galilee to Jerusalem, but without clarifying what this means (v. 31). The emphasis is upon: "the many days"[89] that Jesus spent with the Twelve after the resurrection, qualifying them as Jesus' witnesses to the people. It is noteworthy that Paul does not appeal to his own witness of the resurrection, but refers to the witness of the Twelve. What Paul does is to proclaim that the promise to the fathers is fulfilled, namely, through Jesus' resurrection (vv. 32-33). And this he can say by appealing to the witness of the Twelve. What Paul does is to "bring the good news" (v. 32), while the Twelve are "witnesses."

Thus, there are only a few references in the apostles' speeches to events during Jesus' earthly life, and they are always followed by statements indicating that the Jews are familiar with these events. A direct link between Jesus' earthly life and the witness of the apostles is found only in Acts 10, and even here there is nothing said that the listeners do not already know.

Nevertheless, it is indisputable that Luke has noticeably involved the apostles in Jesus' earthly life. Here he simply follows tradition, even though he has also given more prominence to the apostles than have Mark and Matthew. Even though Luke does not stress the apostles' special knowledge of Jesus and his message in Acts, it is conceivable that because he does this in the Gospel, it is unnecessary to re-emphasize it in Acts. But even in the Gospel the apostles do not know more than others, as is clear when compared with Mark who does mention esoteric instruction.

Mark 4:10ff. deals with the correct understanding of the parables. Here Jesus instructs the Twelve and the other disciples in private about the parables (4:10). Luke omits the comment that this occurs in private; the public scene from Luke 8:4 remains, and the disciples ask Jesus about the meaning of only one of the parables (8:9). Luke also omits the conclusion in Mark 4:34 that Jesus privately instructed his disciples about everything. There is no hint of esoteric instruction in Luke.

The teaching about true greatness (Mark 9:35ff.) is given to the Twelve whom Jesus specifically called together (v. 35). In Luke Jesus speaks to his disciples without reference to the Twelve (9:46). The warning against the leaven of the Pharisees (Mark 8:14ff.) is intentionally directed to the disciples, accusing them of not understanding. Luke places this saying in a scene where a multitude is gathered (12:1, 13), and it is explicitly stated that Jesus spoke first to his disciples (12:1). The disciples' inability to drive out demons (Mark 9:14ff.) is again followed by esoteric instruction (9:28, cf. Matt. 17:19); this instruction is omitted by Luke, who replaces it with a remark about the amazement of the crowd (9:43).

The saying about divorce (Mark 10:2ff.) concludes with special instruction for the disciples (v. 10ff.). In Luke this saying (16:18) stands within the speech about wealth (16:1ff.); according to 16:1 the words are directed to the disciples, but this does not prevent the Pharisees from hearing everything (16:14).

After the question by the rich young man (Mark 10:17ff.) Jesus gives a speech on wealth and discipleship only to his disciples (10:23, 24); in Luke these remarks are public (18:24). The saying concerning the widow's mite (Mark 12:41ff.) is directed to the disciples (v. 43); in Luke it is directed to everyone (21:1ff). Mark and Matthew direct the apocalyptic discourse to the disciples or to an inner circle (13:1, 2, 3, 23); in Luke it is public (21:5, 7). In individual instances Luke has followed the Markan text, but here it has another meaning (cf. Luke 9:10; 10:23; 20:45).

In conclusion: what the apostles know is known not only by other disciples, but by all the people as well.[90] The apostles' knowledge about Jesus' life is not the basis of their position. This agrees with 22:30: as eschatological regents it is not necessary to guarantee the events in Jesus' life.[91] Nor is it commissioning that constitutes the Twelve.[92] Mark explicitly states the purpose in choosing the Twelve: 1) they are to be with Jesus and 2) they will be sent out to preach and to drive out evil spirits (3:14). Luke also notes that the Twelve were with Jesus during his public ministry (8:1), but the same holds true for a number of women who had been healed (8:2). In the first place Luke has separated the choosing from the commissioning (6:12ff. and 9:1). In the second place appointment is not an identifying mark for the Twelve, which is clearly seen in the sending out of the seventy-two (10:1ff.). The seventy-two are sent out with the same mission and the same authority as the Twelve, namely, proclamation of the kingdom of God and power over demons (10:1, 9, 17, cf. 9:1, 2, 6). If it is the concept of the messenger's authority that characterizes the apostolate, then in reality the seventy-two are closer to apostles than the Twelve (see 10:16!).

The significance of pointing out the apostles' connection with Jesus' earthly life can be summarized as follows: First of all, the Twelve must naturally be acquainted with Jesus' earthly life, just as the other disciples are and for that matter the whole Jewish people. They know that the earthly Jesus is the risen Messiah of Israel. The writing of the Gospel and Acts rests on what has been handed down by "eye-witnesses and ministers of the word" (Luke 1:1ff.); here the reference is not to the Twelve, although they are *also* included.

Secondly, it is the earthly Jesus who on God's behalf has chosen the Twelve. Only the Twelve are chosen.[93]

Thirdly, the fulfillment of Scripture regarding Jesus as Israel's Messiah is revealed only to the Twelve (Luke 24:46ff.). In accordance with this Luke emphasizes that it is particularly the Twelve who follow Jesus during his last days in Jerusalem (18:31; 22:3, 8, 14); they have been with the Messiah in his trials (22:28).

Finally, the Twelve were present when Jesus the Messiah delivered his "testament" (Luke 22:29f.): to them has been entrusted the responsibility for Israel.

Notes

[1] For a combination of the Twelve with the conception of the *new* Israel see G. B. Caird, *Saint Luke* (Baltimore: Penguin Books, 1963) 240; S. Brown, "Apostasy and Perseverence in the Theology of Luke," AnBib 26 (1964) 64, 96; J. Fitzmeyer, "Jewish Christianity in Acts in Light of the Qumran Scrolls," *Studies in Luke-Acts,* ed. L. E. Keck and J. L. Martyn (Nashville: Abingdon Press, 1966) 235; B. Gerhardsson, *Memory and Manuscript* (ASNU 22; Uppsala: Gleerup, 1961) 251; T. F. Glasson, *The Second Advent* (London: Epworth Press, 1963) 141ff.; A. J. B. Higgins, *The Lord's Supper in the New Testament* (London: SCM Press, 1952) 11; M. J. Lagrange, *Evangile selon Saint Luc* (Paris: J. Gabalda, 1958) 552; A. R. C. Leaney, *A Commentary on the Gospel according to St. Luke* (London: A & C Black, 1958) 270; Ph.-H. Menoud, "Jesus et ses temoins," *ET* 23 (1960) 7ff.; B. Rigaux, "Die 'Zwölf' in Geschichte und Gegenwart," in *Der historische Jesus und der kerygmatische Christus,* ed. H. Ristow-K. Matthiae (Berlin: Evangelische Verlaganstalt, 1960) 481; H. Schürmann, *Das Lukasevangelium* I (Freiburg: Herder, 1969) 315; J. Wellhagen, *Anden och Riket* (Stockholm: Svenska kyrkans diakonistyrelses bokförlag, 1941) 31; H. D. Wendland, *Die Eschatologie des Reiches Gottes bei Jesus* (Gütersloh: Gütersloher Verlagshaus, 1931) 159.

² G. Klein, *Die zwölf Apostel* (FRLANT 59; Göttingen: Vandenhoeck und Ruprecht, 1961) 205.

³ J. Weiss, *The History of Primitive Christianity,* trans. F. C. Grant (New York: Wilson-Erickson, 1937) II, 687; W. Mundle, "Das Apostelbild der Apostelgeschichte," *ZNW* 27 (1928) 40; J. Roloff, *Apostolat-Verkündigung-Kirche* (Gütersloh: Gütersloher Verlagshaus, 1965) 170.

⁴ Mundle, 40; H. von Campenhausen, *Ecclesial Authority and Spiritual Power,* trans. J. A. Baker (Stanford: Stanford University Press, 1969) 14; E. Schweizer, *Church Order in the New Testament,* trans. F. Clarke (Naperville: A. R. Allenson, 1961) 69f.; H. Conzelmann, *Die Apostelgeschichte* (HNT 7; Tübingen: J. C. B. Mohr (Paul Siebeck), 1963) 54; E. Haenchen, *The Acts of the Apostles,* trans. B. Noble et. al. (Philadelphia: Westminster Press, 1971) 153f.; G. Stählin, *Die Apostelgeschichte* (NTD 5; Göttingen: Vandenhoeck und Ruprecht, 1962) 28.

⁵ H. Conzelmann, *The Theology of St. Luke,* trans. G. Buswell (New York: Harper & Row, 1961) 216; Haenchen, 163, 353; E. Hennecke—W. Schneemelcher, *New Testament Apocrypha,* trans. R. McL. Wilson (Philadelphia: Westminster Press, 1964) II, 29f. Klein, 206; Mundle, 40; Roloff, 233; G. Schrenk, "Verleugnung, Verspottung und Verhör Jesu nach Lukas 22:54-71," ATANT 22 (1969) 205; Schweizer, 69f.; Stählin, 28.

⁶ Roloff, 193: The task of the apostles is mainly proclamation and mission, and not primarily to be "regents within the Jerusalem church"; see however, 170. Contrary to Roloff: Haenchen, 144, n. 1; W. Schmithals, *The Office of Apostle in the Early Church,* trans. J. E. Steely (Nashville: Abingdon Press, 1969) 247f.; J. Wagenmann, *Die Stellung des Apostles Paulus neben der Zwölf in den ersten drei Jahrhunderten* (Giessen: A. Töpelmann, 1926) 66.

⁷ Cf. J. A. Fitzmeyer 235: "A nucleus of twelve . . . symbolizes the fact that the group is the New Israel." Glasson 141ff.: ". . . symbolically the promise of the new Israel"—for which reason every eschatological reference disappears.

⁸ E. Haenchen, *Der Weg Jesu* (Berlin: A. Töpelmann, 1966) 486, claims that it is possible to conclude from Luke 22:30 that Luke uses a Jewish Christian source; cf. also *Acts,* 164; B. S. Easton, *The Gospel according to St. Luke* (New York: Scribner, 1926) 325, sees v. 30 as "a paraphrase of Psa. 122:5"; the language is "intensely Jewish"; on 326 he claims that v. 30 is "too Jewish to refer to Luke." See also

J. M. Creed, *The Gospel according to St. Luke* (London: Macmillan, 1930) 269; H. Schürmann *Eine Quellenkritischen Untersuchung des Lukanischen Abendmahlberichts III, Jesu Abschiedsrede* (Münster: Aschendorffsche Verlagsbuchhandlung, 1956) 42, 47f., also reckons with pre-Lukan material; cf. also 52, 54; Schürmann finds a tendency to reshape the statement from a transferral of power to the twelve to a general consideration of merit.

[9] For a characteristic view: W. Grundmann, *Das Evangelium nach Lukas* (HKNT 3; Berlin: Evangelische Verlagsanstalt, 1966) 445: The disciples entertain false expectations.

[10] Cf. note 8. In his *Theology.*, Conzelmann ignores Luke 22:29f.

[11] There is a certain embarrassment among commentators concerning v. 6. O. Bauernfeind *Die Apostelgeschichte* (HKNT 5; Leipzig: A. Deichert, 1939) 21f., raises the question whether Jesus rejects a relapse into Jewish nationalism, but claims that Luke uses "kingdom to Israel" with a different connotation than elsewhere in Acts, namely, as in Gal. 6:6; Conzelmann, *Apostelgeschichte*, 22, and Haenchen, *Acts*, 143, also claim that the question in v. 6 is raised on the basis of Jewish presuppositions. However, the real problem in the context is the time aspect, not that it concerns the restoration of Israel.

[12] Bibliographic survey: J. Dupont, *Etudes sur les Actes des Apôtres* (LD 45; Paris: Editions du Cerf, 1967) 83ff.

[13] Cf. Below notes 38, 39, 40.

[14] See Roloff, 197—(concerning the Jewish terminology in Acts 1:15ff. cf. 172fl.). Roloff claims that Luke has no interest in connecting the Twelve with the eschatological people of God. Further see: N. Brox, *Zeuge und Märtyrer* (StANT; Müchen: Kösel Verlag, 1961) 50, n. 21; K. H. Rengstorf, "The Election of Matthias," *Current Issues in New Testament Interpretation*, ed. W. Klassen and G. F. Snyder (New York: Scribner, 1962) 191. For a different view: Bauernfeind, *Apostelgeschichte*, 24ff.; see also Tr. Holtz *Untersuchungen über die alttestamentliche Zitate* (Berlin: Akademie Verlag, 1968) 46: The selection of Psalm 109 originates with Luke himself.

[15] Haenchen, 336 views the disappearance of the Twelve from the picture in Acts as "a problem that we . . . find one of the most distressing in Acts." This is a historical problem, but it is not difficult to understand this disappearance from Luke's perspective.

[16] See "The Divided People of God," Part III.

[17] See "The Lost Sheep of the House of Israel."

[18] See "The Law in Luke-Acts," 143-145.

¹⁹ It is well established that Luke equates "the apostles" with "the twelve" and need not be further substantiated here.

²⁰ Cf. passages like 3:7, 10, 21; 4:14f., 23, 37, 44; 5:17; 7:1, 3, 17; 8:4 40; 11:29; 12:1, 54; 13:22; 14:25; 15:1f.; 16:14; 18:18, 36, 43; 19:7, 47, 48; Chapters 20-24 *passim*.

²¹ 2:22, 36; 3:14; 4:10; 10:37f., etc.

²² On the literary relationship between Luke 22:30 and Matt. 19:28: Schürmann, *Jesu Abschiedsrede*, 36 with bibliographical references. Cf. also V. Taylor, *Jesus and his Sacrifice* (London: Macmillan, 1937) 189; Roloff, 186; Rigaux, 476f.

²³J. Munck, "Discours d'adieu dans le Noveau Testament et dans la litterature biblique," in *Aux Sources de la tradition chretienne* (Neuchatel: Delachaux & Niestle, 1950) 154ff.; see also Roloff, 184.

²⁴ It can hardly be doubted that within the framework of a farewell discourse *diathēkē* naturally means "last will and testament." Cf. R. Bultmann, *History of the Synoptic Tradition*, trans. J. Marsh (Oxford: Basil Blackwell, 1963) 159; Schürmann, *Jesu Abschiedsrede*, 41f.; Roloff, 186.

²⁵ Cf. R. Bultmann, *Theology of the New Testament*, trans. K. Grobel (New York: Scribner, 1955) I, 17; von Campenhausen, 16; Grundmann, *Lukas*, 405; Haenchen, *Der Weg Jesus*, 486f.; K. H. Rengstorf, *Das Evangelium nach Lukas* (5th ed.; Göttingen: Vandenhoeck und Ruprecht, 1949) 239; Schürmann, *Jesu Abschiedsrede*, 42; A. Schlatter, *Das Evangelium nach Lukas* (Stuttgart: Calwer Verlag, 1931) 425f., claims that in Luke 22:29f. we encounter again the motif of the king on David's throne in Luke 1-2.

²⁶ There is some disagreement here whether *krinein* means "to judge" or "to rule." For the first opinion see G. Schrenk, *Die Weissagung über Israel im Neuen Testament* (Zürich: Gotthelf Verlag, 1951) 17ff.; K. H. Rengstorf, TDNT II, 327; for the other view: Bultmann, *Theology of the NT*, I, 37; W. G. Kümmel, *Promise and Fulfillment* (Naperville: A. R. Allenson, 1957) 47; A. Fridrichsen, *The Apostle and his Message* (Uppsala: Lundequistska bokhandeln, 1947) 18 n. 2; Haenchen, *Der Weg Jesu*, 486f.; Leaney, 270; E. Stauffer, *New Testament Theology*, trans. J. Marsh (New York: Macmillan, 1961) 308; Taylor, 189; Roloff, 149 comments that the word in Matt. 19:28 means "to judge," while in Luke 22 it means "to rule."

²⁷ E. Hirsh, *Frühgeschichte des Evangeliums* (Tübingen: J. C. B. Mohr (Paul Siebeck), 1941) II, 284, rightly notes that Luke 22:14-38 represents one of Luke's most unique and independent compositions.

[28] Cf. Ph. Seidensticker, *Die Auferstehung Jesu in der Botschaft der Evangelisten* (Stuttgart: Verlag kath. Bibel. werk, 1967), 95f.

[29] G. Klein, "Lukas 1:1-4 als theologisches Programm," in *Zeit und Geschichte,* ed. E. Dinkler (Tübingen: J. C. B. Mohr (Paul Siebeck), 1964) 202f., also claims that 13:31 is concerned exclusively with the apostles. For another view see Haenchen *Acts,* 161: because of the conditions established for the selection of a new apostle (Acts 1:21ff.), it is impossible that 1:3f. and 13:31 refer exclusively to the "apostles."

[30] H. Schürmann, *Das Lukasevangelium,* I, 265, claims that what the apostles lack in order to fulfill their task after the resurrection is the Spirit: cf. also Schmithals, 248, the Spirit is constitutive for the apostolate. For another view, see Conzelmann, *Theology,* 216.

[31] Roloff, 193, finds a typological contrast between the calling of Moses and the apostles; this is in contrast to scholars who find a typological contrast between Moses and Christ: F. Dornseiff, "Lukas der Schriftsteller," *ZNW* 35 (1936) 129f.; J. Manek, "The New Exodus in the Books of Luke," *NovT* 2 (1957) 8ff.; M. Goguel, *La foi a la resurrection de Jesus* (Paris: E. Leroux, 1933) 254.

[32] It is indisputable that *basileia* here can only mean "reign," and not "realm." Cf. G. E. Ladd, *Jesus and the Kingdom* (New York: Harper & Row, 1964) 132.

[33] The statement by P. Richardson, "Israel in the Apostolic Church," *NTS* 10 (1969) 165, is incomprehensible: "At the end of the Gospel (24:21) as at the beginning of Acts (1) he can refer to the hope of 'Israel' not in a transposed sense, but as something which is being lost." What textual basis exists for this? Richardson fails to deal with Luke 22:30 in his exposition of Luke. For 22:30 as a saying of Jesus, see 63, n. 4.

[34] Cf. my essay "The Divided People of God," 51-53.

[35] Roloff, 177, clearly sees that it is God who makes the choice; cf. also B. Lindars, *New Testament Apologetic* (Philadelphia: Westminster Press, 1961) 102f.; for another view see Rengstorf, "The Election of Matthias," 183f.

[36] It must be emphasized that Acts 1:21f. does not say that the apostles are to be witnesses to Jesus' earthly life; their witness is tied exclusively to the resurrection. For the opposing view see Klein, "Lukas 1:1-4," 204. He claims that according to Acts 10:39 the apostles are to bear witness to Jesus' earthly life; 1:22 is concerned with the resurrection, and both are included in the witness of the apostles.

[37] Concerning the casting of lots: W. A. Beardsley, "The Casting of Lots at Qumran and in the Book of Acts," *NovT* 4 (1960) 245ff.; cf. also Pauly-Wissowa XIII, 1451f.; further Schweizer, 70, n. 261; C. H. Dodd, *According to the Scriptures* (London: Nisbet, 1958) 58, n. 1; E. Stauffer, "Jüdisches Erbe im urchristlichen Kirchenrecht," *TLZ* 77 (1952) 201ff.; J. Renie "L'election de Mathias (Acts 1, 15-26) authenticite du recit," *RB* 55 (1948) 43ff.

[38] Roloff, 196, claims that Acts 1:15-26 is not the starting point for a reconstruction of the Lukan picture of the apostles, but rather Luke 22:29 (not v. 30!), cf. 187.—This appears to be an artificial division of texts, and does not enhance the understanding.

[39] Roloff, 177; Conzelmann, *Apostelgeschichte,* 25; Haenchen, *Acts,* 164.

[40] Klein, *Apostel,* 206.

[41] According to Klein *(ibid.)* it plays no role for Luke.

[42] Thus Klein, see n. 40.

[43] Lindars, 187, claims that the Twelve in Luke 22:30 are given a "formal position" over the twelve tribes, and thereby a mission to the entire people is indicated, while, "In the first chapters of Acts this formal constitution . . . appears as a curious survival." Somewhat more cautious is Schweizer, 28f. n. 70. Some of the eschatological import of Luke 22:29 may carry over into Acts, although Schweizer thinks it is unimportant for Luke.

[44] Roloff, 187, finds that Luke 22:29 is the key to Luke's picture of the apostles. Typical for Roloff's understanding is the disappearance of v. 30 from the picture, and the silence about the relationship between the Twelve and Israel. Nor will Roloff view the apostles primarily as "the first regents within the Jerusalem church," (193) because their task according to 1:8 consists of proclamation and mission. For Klein *(Apostel,* 204f.) Acts 1:21f. is the determining passage. On the other hand, Luke 22:29f. cannot be of any significance for Klein since he does not deal with it in his discussion of Luke. 22:30 concerns "a function of the office of kingship," Kümmel, 47; in addition see those who are named in n. 25 above and also Fridrichsen, 18, n. 12; Stauffer, *NT Theology,* n. 637.

[45] On the issue of authenticity, for the negative view cf. J. Weiss, *The History of Primitive Christianity,* 47f.; R. Bultmann, *History of the Synoptic Tradition,* 158f.; V. Taylor, *The Gospel according to St. Mark* (London: Macmillan, 1952) 51, n. 3; for the other view: Roloff,

148f.; Kümmel, 41; Schürmann, *Jesu Abschiedsrede,* 42; Rigaux, 476; On the relationship between the Matthean and Lukan versions see Taylor, *Sacrifice.,* 188; Roloff, 186.

[46] Thus also Brown, 84; Lagrange, 552; H. E. Tödt, *The Son of Man in the Synoptic Tradition,* trans. D. M. Barton (Philadelphia: Westminster Press, 1965) 64, claims that because the promise is not given to the Twelve, but to all the disciples, the comment that there are twelve thrones is lacking; Taylor, *Sacrifice.,* 189, considers the possibility that Luke could have excluded the number twelve in an attempt to ameliorate the statement's "awkwardness."

[47] Cf. the comment in Lindars, 102f. It is characteristic for Acts "that traditions of exegesis are often much more primitive than their context, or their actual form, seems to suggest."

[48] Cf. F. Schütz, *Der Leidende Christus* (BWANT 9; Stuttgart: W. Kohlhammer, 1969) 123; T. Schramm, *Der Markusstoff bei Lukas* (Hamburg: 1966) 82f.

[49] Schütz, 123.

[50] Similarly Schürmann, *Das Lukasevangelium.,* I, 313.

[51] Grundmann, *Lukas,* 249.

[52] Concerning scriptural interpretation see Lindars, 102ff.; for scriptural proof and exegesis for the resurrection, 32-74. For a general Lukan interpretation of scripture see M. Rese, *Alttestamentliche Motive in der Christologie des Lukas* (Bonn: 1965); Holtz; E. Lövestam, *Son and Saviour,* trans. M. J. Petry (Lund: Gleerup, 1961)—on Acts 13:32-37.

[53] Lindars 102f., claims that Psa. 69:26 is already "the technical grounds for electing a new apostle." For an opposing view, see Haenchen, *Acts,* 161.

[54] Haenchen, "Judentum und Christentum in der Apostelgeschichte," *ZNW* 54 (1963) 162, finds it characteristic for Luke that Acts 1:15ff. does not refer back to Luke 22:30 but motivates the choice by citing Psa. 109:8.

[55] Rengstorf, "The Election of Matthias," 183f., interprets this as a reference to the Risen One. Similarly Rigaux, 481; cf. also Gaechter, *ZKT* (1949) 318ff. For another view: Roloff, 177. Concerning the idea of God as "the one who knows the heart": *Herm. Mand.* IV 3, 4; *Acta Pauli et Theclae* 24; *Apost. Const.* II 24, 6; III 7, 8; IV 6, 8; VI 12, 4; VIII 5, 6; Clem. Alex. *Strom.* V 14, 16.

[56] Cf. Klein, "Lukas 1:1-4," 203, especially n. 62.

[57] See 22:14 and 26:16 concerning the divine foreordination of Paul.

[58] Rengstorf, 185, views the choice of a new apostle as a confession

of Jesus' messiahship. The crucifixion was not a messianic catastrophe. Thus Rengstorf has undoubtedly seen something important in the text. It is more difficult to understand that this viewpoint according to Rengstorf is not Lukan.

[59] For the view that Matt. 19:28 is weakened in relation to Luke 22:30 see Schürmann, *Jesu Abschiedsrede*, 37 and 41; in Matthew it is a "promise of reward" for all the disciples, while in Luke it is a "transfer of authority" to the Twelve.

[60] Haenchen, *Acts*, 164.

[61] Lindars, 187.

[62] Luke uses *Christos* with a technical meaning; Rese, 184ff.; F. Hahn, *The Titles of Jesus in Christology*, trans. H. Knight and G. Ogg (London: Lutterworth Press, 1969) 187f.; J. C. O'Neill, *The Theology of Acts in its Historical Setting* (London: S. P. C. K. 1961) 117ff., attempts to explain the technical use: "the peculiarities of Lucan use of "Christ" should be explained against a background of Christian and Jewish disputes in the second century about the identity of the Messiah" (123). However, the dating of Luke in the second century is impossible. For Luke it is essential to clarify that Jesus actually is *Israel's Messiah*. Therefore he is the only one of the New Testament authors who in this context takes a closer look at the word *Chriein*, Luke 4:18; Acts 4:27; 10:38.

[63] Neither Matthew nor Mark have introduced Scripture in connection with the passion statements; nor is this done by Luke in 9:22 or 24:7. In Luke 9:44 the resurrection is not mentioned at all. Luke's reworking of the tradition (18:31ff.; 24:25-27, 32, 44-46) shows how he would have understood the statements.

[64] Grundmann, *Lukas*, 404. The notion of the Christians as co-regents is widespread in early Christianity. However, it is characteristic for Luke to limit this notion to the Twelve.

[65] Klein, "Lukas 1:1-4," 207ff., has tried to show that the infancy narrative is also presupposed in the Lukan prologue.

[66] Concerning the understanding of Jesus as a Jewish king, i.e. the national-political element in Luke, see H. Cadbury, *The Making of Luke-Acts* (New York: Macmillan, 1927) 277f. "More than any other New Testament writer Luke brings to our sight the current Messianic hopes of Judaism." Cadbury comments, however, that Luke "can scarcely have ever held this political view of the matter himself. . . ." Considering that Luke writes with Jewish Christians in mind, this element in his theology is understandable.

[67] Conzelmann, *Theology.*, 166, claims that the Old Testament figures play no role in Luke's historical schema. For another view, see N. A. Dahl, "The Story of Abraham in Luke-Acts," *Studies in Luke-Acts,* ed. L. E. Keck and J. L. Martyn (Nashville: Abingdon Press, 1966) 139: ". . . [Luke] considers the history of Israel to be bound up with individual persons, of whom Abraham, Moses, and David are the most outstanding."

[68] According to Acts 4:2 the apostles do not witness to Jesus' resurrection *per se,* but to the resurrection in Jesus, "proclaiming in Jesus the resurrection from the dead," i.e. Israel's hope. On this verse see Haenchen, *Acts,* 214f. and Bauernfeind, 74.

[69] See J. Jervell, "Midt i Israels historie," *NTT* (1968) 130ff.

[70] Concerning the relationship between Acts 10:42 and 1:8 see Bauernfeind, 150.—There is no reason to see any opposition between the "missionary mandate" in 1:8 and 10:42 as long as it remains clear that the admittance of the Gentiles is the fulfillment of the promise to Israel.

[71] According to Rengstorf, "The Election of Matthias," 188f., the historical function of the Twelve is fulfilled with the completion of the full circle of the Twelve; thereby Jesus' claim on Israel as his people is made clear. Rengstorf touches on something important here, but his view can hardly be carried through consistently. Even though the Twelve are mentioned explicitly only a few times in Acts, we can not overlook the importance of Luke's identification of the apostles with the Twelve. Conzelmann, *Apostelgeschichte,* 121, views the Apostolic Council as a turning point, namely as the transition to the post-apostolic epoch, which is represented in Jerusalem by James. It is difficult to understand that this can really be the case, since James hardly seems to play any role as an "epochal" figure in Acts, cf. my essay "James: the Defender of Paul."

[72] Cf. Schütz, 125.

[73] The Twelve are relatively insignificant as missionaries: Haenchen, *Acts,* 144, n. 1.

[74] It is difficult to understand how U. Wilckens, *Die Missionsreden der Apostelgeschichte* (Neukirchen: Neukirchener Verlag, 1961) 44ff., can characterize the speeches in Acts 4:9ff. and 5:30ff. as "missionary speeches."

[75] Cf. "The Divided People of God," Part III.

[76] See N. A. Dahl, "A People for His Name." *NTS* 4 (1957) 319ff. For Conzelmann, *Apostelgeschichte,* 83, the verse is a "clearly para-

doxical formulation." See also J. Dupont, "Laos ek ethnōn," *NTS* 3 (1956) 47ff.

[77] Easton, *St. Luke,* 325, claims in connection with Luke 22:30 that "the Kingdom contains only Israel." But Easton has isolated the statement within Lukan theology.

[78] There are good reasons for taking up anew the question of Luke's ecclesiology. Luke's view is unique within the New Testament. Technical ecclesiological terms common at the time Luke wrote are lacking in Acts. A concordance clearly shows that Luke has used *ekklēsia,* but he employs it with non-technical use. *Ekklēsia* can stand for any kind of a gathering of people, a riotous meeting (19:32, 39, 40) or for Israel in the wilderness (7:38). "God's *ekklēsia*" is not Luke's expression; it is used only with reference to the Old Testament (20:28). The word is missing where it would appear to be necessary (2:41, 47; 5:14; 11:24), i.e. where it has been inserted by individual scribes (cf. 2:47). Typically, *oikos* stands for Israel (2:36; 7:42, 46); *adelphoi* may be used of the believers, but the characteristic use is for Jews, never non-Jews (cf. 1:16; 2:29, 37; 3:17, 22; 7:2; 13:15, 26, 38; 22:1, 5; 23:1, 5, 6; 28:17). "Descendents of Abraham" are always Israel, never the believers among Jews and Gentiles, and Abraham is the father of the Jews, not of the believers (Luke 1:55, 73; 13:16; 19:9; Acts 3:13, 25; 7:2, 5f., 16, 17, 32; 13:26). "The twelve tribes of Israel" are Israel, not the church (Luke 22:30; Acts 10:28; 26:7). The mention of "the fathers" is also typical; from tradition Luke knows the use of "the fathers" as those who killed the prophets, but his typical use of "the fathers" occurs in the expression "the promise to the fathers"; they are the fathers of the historical Israel, the Jews (Luke 1:55, 72; Acts 3:25; 7:8; 13:32; see further Acts 13:17, 23; cf. 2:39).

[79] See above n. 3.

[80] Cf. Rengstorf, "The Election of Matthias," 182; see also Conzelmann, *Theology,* 217f. Other views are represented by such scholars as Wellhausen, J. Weiss, and Reicke.

[81] Cf. Dahl, "The Story of Abraham," 152f., concerning the idea behind Luke's writing of history: ". . . his own conscious intention was to write history in biblical style or, rather, to write the continuation of the biblical history."

[82] Schweizer, *Gemeinde,* 69ff.

[83] Wagenmann, 74, interprets it at this point to mean "transfer of office." See also Schmithals, 249.

[84] E. Haenchen, *Acts,* 262.

[85] See above n. 5.

[86] Concerning these sayings, Schütz, 135ff., says that Luke's intention is not to polemicize against "the Jews."

[87] If the knowledge of Jesus' preaching to the Twelve after the resurrection is the decisive criterion, then according to Acts 1:3f. Matthias stands in a strange position. For strictly speaking, he lacks the necessary prerequisites to be chosen as an apostle as set forth in Acts 1:21. The same problem appears in Acts 10:41 and 13:31. On this question see Klein, "Lukas 1:1-4," 202ff., who maintains that in these passages Luke is no longer considering the new selection (204). However, it is impossible to say whether Luke was aware of the problem.

[88] Conzelmann *Apostelgeschichte*, 77, claims that "the witnesses" include more than the twelve. For a different view see Haenchen, *Acts*, 411 and Klein, 202f. Wagenmann, 68f., points out that Acts 1:3 is intended primarily to show that the apostles are alone accorded full recognition and can interpret Jesus' message. However, Wagenmann too hastily combines 1:3 with Luke 24:25.

[89] Clearly this is the same as the forty days in Acts 1:3. Concerning this and the number in Christian tradition see Conzelmann *Apostelgeschichte*, 20f.

[90] Against this one cannot cite Luke 1:1-4 as evidence that what Luke writes in his Gospel goes back to the Twelve alone, since they "from the beginning were eye witnesses and ministers of the word." Klein, "Lukas 1:1-4" 210ff., tries to show that Luke 1:2 can only refer to the Twelve. Throughout Klein's discussion the question remains why Luke in his prologue did not insert "the Twelve" or "the apostles," but is content with statements which do not set them off from other "ministers of the word." See also E. Güttgemans, *Offene Fragen zur Formgeschichte des Evangeliums* (München: C. Kaiser, 1970) 192.

[91] Klein, "Lukas 1:1-4," 204, claims that the apostles' testimony concerns Jesus' earthly life and resurrection, and both parts are included in the concept "witness." Concerning Jesus' life, Klein refers only to Acts 10:39 and assumes that both earthly life and resurrection are meant in Acts 1:8 and 13:31. However, neither of these passages furnishes any evidence for his assumption, especially since in Acts 1:21 the witness deals only with the resurrection.

[92] Cf. Conzelmann, *Theology*, 216.

[93] Schütz, 123, maintains that the election is decisive.

The Lost Sheep of the House of Israel

The Understanding
of the Samaritans
in Luke-Acts

I

Among the New Testament writers it is Luke who takes most interest in the Samaritans. This is striking since Luke according to general opinion is a Gentile Christian with an explicitly universalistic inclination. As is well known, the New Testament, except for the Lukan writings, rarely deals with the Samaritan people and their religion.[1]

The fourth chapter of John's Gospel relates the story of the Samaritan woman.[2] The account indicates that the gospel writer knows something about the Samaritans' relation to the Christian faith. The comment in 4:9c makes it clear that the readers of the gospel know very little about the Samaritans; the readers must be supplied with information about the relationship between Jews and Samaritans. The redactional stage from which this comment is derived is unimportant.[3] Furthermore, John 8:48 reveals an awareness of the Jewish disdain for the Samaritans. The obvious point in John's account is that the Samaritans are not Jews, as is clear in 4:9 and 22.

Matthew 10:5 contains a short missionary directive that betrays a Jewish or Jewish Christian attitude toward the Samaritans. In Matthew as well, it is obvious that the Samaritans are not Jews, for here the "house of Israel" is contrasted with the Samaritans and the Gentiles.[4]

Except for the scattered references just cited, there is no material about the Samaritans in the New Testament apart from Luke. If we can infer from John and Matthew that there is some knowledge of the Samaritans in Christian circles,[5] then at least one point is clear—that the Samaritans are not Jews.[6]

In contrast to the other New Testament writers, Luke includes extensive material of various literary types about the Samaritans. It is so extensive that it betrays an interest in the Samaritans above and beyond traditional usage. Luke includes a parable (10:25-37), a miracle (17:11-19), and a lengthy historical account of the evangelization of Samaria (Acts 8:4ff.). Finally, a number of references occur at important points in the narrative: Luke 9:52ff.; Acts 1:8; 8:1; 9:31 and 15:3.

The inclusion of this material in a supposedly universalistic writing is not in itself surprising. It is even conceivable that Luke used the Samaritans precisely to demonstrate universalism: to show how the gospel burst the boundaries of Judaism. There are two considerations that clearly demonstrate, however that this has not been his purpose.

First, Luke does not view the gospel as addressed to mankind in general, or to mankind without a nationality or history, but to men whose history is Israel's as the chosen people. Luke does not share Matthew's view of making disciples of all nations; he does not view the church as a church of all peoples.[7] His understanding lies closer to the Pauline "to the Jew first and also to the Greek." Luke consistently operates within the limits of the conception "Israel" and "the nations." However, within this framework the Samaritans have been accorded a place.

Second, a form critical analysis indicates that Luke does not use the Samaritan material in an illustrative way for Gentile Christian readers, as we shall see below. It is conceivable that Luke the historian has heard about the Christian mission in Samaria, and thus includes this material within his description of the "spreading of the word" from Jerusalem to the "ends of the earth" simply because it is available to him.[8]

However, it is obvious that Luke's interest in the Samaritans is not merely "archivistic," prompted by the tradition. In Acts 8 we encounter more than a source and a tradition taken over by Luke without revision. A first consideration is that the language and style are no different from what is acknowledged as typically Lukan. A more important consideration is that Luke himself has associated the Jerusalem apostles with the mission in Samaria (8:14ff.). From an analysis of the composition in Acts 8, it is readily apparent that this association was not inherent in the material from the beginning.[9] In addition, Acts 8 contains a number of theological comments concerning mission, clearly stemming from the author's hand. The Samaritans are mentioned in these comments: Acts 1:8; 9:31 and 15:3. Finally, there are detailed stories in Luke's special material (Luke 10 and 17), which indicate a particular interest in the Samaritans. Perhaps what is most important is that in composing his Gospel, Luke has inserted the Samaritan episode (9:52ff.) into the Markan outline. Even if this short account should be pre-Lukan, which is doubtful[10], it would not be decisive for interpretation. What is decisive is that Luke himself has inserted this narrative at an important turning point in his story.

It is also important to observe that Luke obviously presupposes among his readers a great deal of knowledge about and familiarity with the Samaritans. He never needs to inform the readers about who or what the Samaritans are. Therefore we lack explanatory notes such as John 4:9 (cf. also 4:20).

A hasty reading of the Lukan material shows that Luke's

account is simply incomprehensible for a reader who knows nothing of the Samaritans. For a reader who is unaware of the relationship between Gerazim and Jerusalem, the introduction to the "travel narrative" (9:51ff.) is unintelligible. How could anyone without such previous knowledge understand, for example, v. 53? And really just what kind of outsiders are the Samaritans? They may be a people like the Gentiles; they may be a Jewish sect or party, or possibly even a place on the map.

Luke 10:30ff. is even less informative. The triad, priest-Levite-Samaritan, is unusual even to a modern exegete and appears meaningless.[11] For a reader, "Samaritan" could just as well designate a type of office holder as a layman. But anyone who is aware of the view that the Samaritans were lax in keeping the law may detect the thrust of the story.[12]

From the story in Luke 17:11ff. an uninformed reader might conclude that the Samaritan was a Gentile (v. 18).[13] But then it remains unintelligible for the reader how Jesus could send this Gentile along with the nine Jews to the Temple in Jerusalem to perform the rites of purification (v. 14).[14]

The "missionary mandate"[15] in Acts 1:8 also adds little to our information about the Samaritans. The sequence—Jerusalem, Judea, Samaria, "to the end of the earth"—would suggest that Samaria is conceived as part of Jewish territory. Further support may be found in 9:31: Judea, Galilee, and Samaria.

Acts 8:4ff. supplies the reader with some information, but in such a way that it tells little about the Samaritans themselves. We learn nothing about their religion or beliefs. Only one real piece of information is given: the Samaritans are a nation (8:9). But nothing is mentioned about what kind of nation they are.[16] The rest of the passage is concerned with Simon Magus and Philip, in other words with events taking place in Samaritan territory.

Viewed as a whole, it seems clear that no uninformed reader

could understand Luke's references to the Samaritans. Of course, it is conceivable that Luke did not care whether his readers had the requisite knowledge to understand these references. But this view does not harmonize with what is said in the prologue (Luke 1:1ff.). Yet if Luke writes for a Jewish Christian audience, then it is easy to understand why he is unconcerned with informing his readers. Obviously they already know about the kind of people referred to as Samaritans.

II

Scholars have focused little attention on the role of the Samaritans within Luke's theological perspective. This is true even of redaction critics.[17] As a rule one definite point of view dominates these studies: Luke regards the Samaritans as Gentiles. Missionary activity in Samaria is therefore the first step in the direction of the mission among the Gentiles.[18]

This approach solves few problems, but it raises new ones. If Luke regards the Samaritans as Gentiles, why has he singled out a particular group of Gentiles? There is no support in the text for understanding the Samaritans as Gentiles or the missionary activity in Samaria as a transition to a purely Gentile mission. This interpretation is supported neither by the details of the text nor by the structure of Luke's composition.

A comparison of Acts 8 with Acts 10-11 shows first of all that the Samaritans are not considered Gentiles.[19] In several ways Luke shows what a decisive event it was when the gospel first reached the Gentiles (10-11): As a Jew Peter does something unheard of (*athemiton*) by associating with or visiting a non-Jew(*allophylos*) (10:28a), because a non-Jew is impure (10:28b)—a verse that points back to Peter's vision (10:10ff.). Strong criticism is leveled against Peter in Jerusalem; the apostles and the brothers accuse Peter because he has had contact with the uncircumcised, with Gentiles (11:1-3, 18). It is easy to see the function of Acts 10-11 in the work as a whole. Here the decisive step is taken in which the nations are included with Israel in the Christian mission.[20]

By placing the Samaritan mission in Chapter 8, that is, prior to the pericope on the Gentiles, Luke shows that the Samaritans were not considered Gentiles. Other observations also indicate that Luke does not make any direct connection between the Samaritan mission and the Gentile mission, that is, Luke makes no attempt to join Chapter 8 to Chapters 10-11 as he does elsewhere when he wants to indicate a connection between chapters. For example, he links Chapters 10-11 to 15 in 15:7, 14 and Chapters 1-7 to 8 in 8:14ff. The details in Chapter 8 lend further support to this interpretation. Philip's missionary activity (8:4ff.) takes place without any mention of difficulties like those reported in Chapters 10-11. No suspicions are awakened in Jerusalem when Samaria accepts the word of God (8:14). On the contrary, Peter and John are sent to Samaria and are instrumental in bringing God's Spirit to the Samaritans, after which they preach in their cities (8:14ff., 25). Obviously, Samaria is not regarded as either Gentile or half-Gentile territory.

The missionary activity in Samaria is a result of the persecution of the congregation in Jerusalem after the death of Stephen (8:2, 4). Samaria's missionary, Philip, is also one of the seven "deacons," the circle around Stephen (6:5). The missionary activity carried on by those driven out is also mentioned in a summary statement (11:19f.). Here it is emphasized that they carried on their mission exclusively among the Jews (v. 19).[21] The first time these refugees from Jerusalem encounter the Gentiles it is noted both who spoke to the Greeks, namely, the men of Cyprus and Cyrene, and where it took place, namely, in Antioch (v. 20). Here, too, it is obvious that for Luke the Samaritans are Jews, or at least they are not Gentiles.

Further confirmation is found in Acts 15.[22] According to Luke, the main purpose of the Apostolic Council is to consider the Gentiles' relationship to the law of Moses, particularly in regard to circumcision (15:1, 5). Here we ought to be aware that for Luke circumcision is not one ritual commandment among others. Circumcision has special importance, because it is an identifying mark of Israel as the people of God (see especially Acts 7:8).[23] Twice in the course of Chapter 15, which deals with the Gentiles' relation to circumcision, mission reports concerning Gentile conversion are made (v. 3, 12). It is explicitly noted that reports of the conversion of the uncircumcised were made to the brothers in Samaria among others (15:3). Obviously the ones receiving the report are themselves circumcised, standing on the same level as the Jews. Since Luke considers circumcision an identifying mark for Israel as the people of God, he clearly includes the Samaritans within the people of God. Samaria is regularly included in Luke's reports of the spread of the mission (1:8), but the Samaritans are not mentioned in the discussions about Gentiles and circumcision (Acts 15).

It is conceivable that Luke refers to a "genuine" Jewish population living in Samaria. He could have pictured the missionary activity as having taken place among the genuine Jews in Samaria and not among the full-fledged Samaritans. This understanding, however, is rendered impossible by two statements in which Luke lets it be known that he deals with the Samaritans as a separate group of people (Luke 17:18; Acts 8:9).[24]

Hans Conzelmann has emphasized how Luke makes it clear that Jesus during his earthly ministry does not move beyond Israel's borders.[25] The one exception that is found, namely Luke 8:26ff., confirms the rule. In connection with the so-called Lukan travel narrative Conzelmann tries to show that

Jesus did not even set foot on Samaritan territory. At most he was in the border areas of Samaria.[26]

Obviously Conzelmann has pointed out an important feature of Luke's Gospel. It can hardly be doubted that it is important for Luke to dissociate Jesus from Gentile territory. The motivation for this scarcely lies in a view of salvation history as composed of epochs or periods,[27] but rather in Luke's theology of mission. Salvation concerns Israel and is extended to and received by Israel as the presupposition for the incoming of the Gentiles. Nevertheless, Conzelmann's observation retains its validity. However, his geographical perspective is doubtful, namely, that Luke imagined that Judea bordered on both Samaria and Galilee.[28] Thereby Jesus could have gone from Galilee to Judea without actually walking in Samaritan territory. One factor that shapes Conzelmann's view is that he considers the Samaritans to be Gentiles or at least non-Jews. But if Luke views the Samaritans as Jews or a kind of Jews who actually have rights of citizenship in Israel, then there is no problem with Jesus' visit in Samaritan territory.

It should be possible to show that this is actually the case. Luke is not content simply to dissociate Jesus from Gentile territory. He also notes that Jesus had no contact with Gentiles in Jewish territory.[29] Luke 7:1ff. is a typical example. It is striking that Luke must give a detailed apology and justification for Jesus' dealings with the Gentile soldier. Jesus acts only when the Jewish elders intercede for the officer (v. 3-5); his love for Israel, his kind deeds to the people, and his piety have entitled him to the healing Jesus can give. According to Matthew 8:5ff. the Roman soldier himself comes directly to Jesus and carries on a conversation with him. Luke does not permit him any direct contact with Jesus. The whole episode unfolds without a meeting between the two main characters.[30]

When Jesus heals a non-Jew, or rather listens to and grants

a prayer from a Gentile, Luke must offer a defense, by referring to the Gentile's close relationship to Israel (7:5). Luke's
concern is obviously not to heighten the miraculous element.[31]
The Jewish leaders who appear play quite another role, and
they would be unnecessary if this were his intention. Luke's
reworking of this account shows that it is hardly accidental
that he does not retell the story of the healing of the Canaanite
woman (Mark 7:25ff; Matt. 15:21ff.) It is not sufficient merely
to mention that the account lies within "the great omission."
Rather it is all too clear that Luke consciously wants to limit
Jesus' activity to the Jews. And it is evident in this context
that Luke has no problem with the Samaritans.

Regardless of how the Lukan "travel narrative" is to be
understood geographically, Luke 9:51-56 shows that Jesus
found himself in Samaritan territory,[32] and that he wished to
be accepted there. Furthermore, in comments (13:32; 17:11)
and also in narratives (10:30ff.; 17:11ff.) Luke gives the impression that Jesus travelled through Samaria.[33] It is also important to note that the portion of the Gospel of Luke that is
described as the "travel narrative" begins with the rejection of
Jesus by the Samaritans. Jesus is rejected because he is going
to Jerusalem; in other words, the rejection motif is related to
Luke's portrayal of Jesus as an orthodox Jew.[34] Gentiles are
never said to reject Jesus or the apostles in Acts. The rejection
motif appears only in connection with the Jews.[35]

Consider also Luke 17:11-19. Luke keeps Jesus at a distance
from Gentiles, but here he does not hesitate to portray him in
close contact with a Samaritan. The contrast to Luke 7:1ff. is
clear. The story in 17:11ff. shows also that Luke considers the
Samaritans as belonging to the Jewish cult; Jesus directs him
to the priests (v. 14). With Luke's understanding of the law
and the cult, it is inconceivable that he could have directed
the Samaritan to a specifically Samaritan cult, "heretical" in
relation to orthodox Judaism.

The geographical references to the progress of the mission also show that for Luke Samaria is Jewish territory: Acts 1:8;[36] 8:1; 9:31. Here Galilee, Judea, and Samaria constitute a unity separated from the rest of the world where "the nations" are found. In Acts 1:8 the border is drawn between Samaria and "the ends of the earth"; Acts 9:31 makes it clear that before any missionary activity occurs in Gentile territory the "church" existed in Judea, Galilee, and Samaria. According to Acts 10:37 the preaching of the good news took place throughout the whole of Judea. This is an explicit reference to the Gospel, and it is obvious that both Galilee and Samaria are included.[37] Acts 10:39 says that the apostles are witnesses to everything Jesus did "in the country of the Jews and Jerusalem"—in which Samaria once again is included. Acts 13:31 explains the role of the apostles in such a way that they are witnesses "to the people"; against the background of the role of the apostles in the earlier parts of Acts we see that this also includes the Samaritans.

There is nothing in Acts to indicate that the Samaritan mission is to be understood as the first step in the mission to the Gentiles. It is no more a transition to the Gentile mission than the activity in Jerusalem is a transition. In the composition of Acts, Chapter 8 belongs together with the preceding material, that is, the activity in Jewish territory. If we are to speak of transitions to the Gentile mission, we must look to the initial activity among the Gentile Godfearers, in other words among people who keep the law and live in close contact with Israel— but without being circumcised. The prototype is Cornelius (10:2-4, 22, 31, 35).

There is still one more point to observe. Acts 10-11 does not mean that from now on the mission activity in Acts deals with the Gentiles. Throughout the entire work, Luke, for good reasons, is concerned with the activity among the Jews. The story focuses upon Jerusalem in Chapters 2-7 and then turns to missionary work in Galilee, Judea, and Samaria in Chapters 8-9. Throughout the rest of the book Luke is occupied with the mission in the Jewish diaspora, while the Gentiles appear only in conjunction with the synagogue and even then at the periphery. The actual Gentile mission first begins at the conclusion of Acts (28:28.) Luke does not intend to write about how the Gentile mission progressed. When all the Jews have heard the gospel, the work begins among the Gentiles. This is because the Gentiles' access to Israel's salvation must await the fulfillment of the promise that the people be gathered. From this perspective as well, it is meaningless to speak about a Samaritan mission as a transition to the Gentile mission.

III

There ought to be no doubt that Luke regards the Samaritans as Jews.[38] Luke's interest in them and explicit references to them are related to their special status within Israel.

This becomes apparent the first time Luke mentions them (Luke 9:51-56). A Samaritan village rejects Jesus. The reason is that Jesus is on the way to Jerusalem, to "his father's house." [39] The significance of this reference for Luke does not lie in the historical information that the Samaritans have an unfriendly attitude toward Jerusalem. The reference is significant because Jerusalem and the temple have a determinative theological significance for Luke.[40] Jerusalem and the temple are the setting for the crucial events in Israel's history, namely the messianic event. We may express it in this way: If the events in the life of Jesus are not concentrated around Jerusalem and the temple, then Jesus, for Luke, is not Israel's Messiah nor is the church Israel. Sections in Luke's Gospel such as 1-2, 23-24, and Acts 1:27 indicate the significance of Jerusalem. Here the coming of the Messiah is prophesied and proclaimed; here the promise of the Davidic Messiah and thereby salvation for Israel is fulfilled. Jerusalem is central for Jesus and the Twelve because Jesus himself and later on the Twelve on Israel's thrones make a claim on Israel.

Against this background the Samaritans' attitude becomes clear. They reject Jesus' or the church's Jewish "orthodoxy." Thus, for Luke they are Jews who have gone astray. They are not the only group within Israel who are in this situation. The Sadducees for Luke are undoubtedly a part of Israel, yet not genuine Jews. This is clearly apparent from their denial of belief in the resurrection, for the resurrection is Israel's hope (Acts 23:1ff.)

Luke also recognizes that within Israel the Samaritans have a special ethnic status. This is seen, among other places, in the statement in Luke 17:18 where the Samaritan leper is called a foreigner (*allogenēs*).[41] By itself this does not mean that they are non-Israelites in a purely ethnic sense, even though this is the usual use of the term in the Septuagint. It is most important that this special ethnic status does not exclude them from Israel in the same manner as proselytes are not excluded from Israel. It is possible that Luke saw the Samaritans as a kind of proselytes,[42] but this concept is in no way developed by him. It is significant that in no context are they reckoned among "the nations" as these are contrasted with Israel.

As we have already shown, the mission in Samaria is a Jewish mission. Therefore no special justification is needed for the mission to Samaria as is necessary in regard to Cornelius. According to the introduction to Chapter 8, the mission to the Samaritans arose when the persecution in Jerusalem forced the congregation into Judea and Samaria (8:1). It ought to be evident that both of these areas should be designated as Jewish. Nothing is reported about a special mission in Judea. What necessitates the mission in Samaria is that here the concern is with the Jews who have gone astray, which is indicated by their relationship to Simon Magus (Acts 8:9ff.).

The entire Samaritan population has been deceived by the magic of the sorcerer and has made a kind of messianic confession to him (8:10-11). "Magic" has an exclusively negative connotation in Luke.

Nowhere can Luke report greater triumphs for the gospel than in Samaria. Furthermore, Luke previously has reported several mass conversions among Jews in Jerusalem (2:41; 4:4; 5:14; 6:1, 7). These comments about mass conversions, however, are always associated with the rejection of the gospel by a segment of the population. In Samaria it is different. Here, too, the masses accept the gospel and give themselves wholeheartedly to it (8:6). But Luke goes beyond that. Simon Magus has deceived the entire population (8:9-11), but this entire population is baptized by Philip (8:12). Thus, for Luke Samaria is a Christian territory. This in turn implies that for Luke all Samaria has also become an "orthodox" Jewish territory. The reason for the obvious interest in the Samaritans should be located here.[43]

It is well known that in other places Luke shows an interest for the outcasts, the poor, and the down-trodden. But we should note that Luke's interest is not bound up with a kind of general philanthropy. It is not mankind, but the down-trodden in Israel in whom Luke is interested. One place where this is evident is in the special Lukan material (Luke 13:16 and 19:9-10).[44] Concern for the outcast in Israel may also lie behind the Samaritan situation, although at a deeper level. From Luke's perspective, Jesus has solved the Samaritan problem; the church has brought the straying Samaritans back to Israel. To put it another way, at the Apostolic Council in Jerusalem James can speak about the restored Israel in which the Gentiles will also be included (15:16ff).[45] This can only be accomplished after the Jews in Samaria have been included in God's promises and their fulfillment. It is important for Luke that the Jewish population of the whole world be con-

fronted with the gospel. By the end of Acts the gospel has
been proclaimed to Jews in all the world. It is clear that in this
context Luke has to include the Samaritans. Their conversion
signifies that they have become "good" Jews, that is, they have
returned to Israel.

This is apparent in a number of passages. In Luke 9:51ff.
the Samaritans reject Jesus because of his close connections
with Jerusalem, while in Acts the Samaritans are closely connected to Jerusalem. In the first place Philip comes from the
church that frequents the temple and is zealous for the law—
because this church is the restored Israel. Furthermore, 8:14-17
reports that the apostles in Jerusalem send Peter and John to
the converts in Samaria. This passage is customarily interpreted ecclesiologically. The church in Samaria is legitimate
only if it is sanctioned by Jerusalem.[46] It is true that here the
Samaritans are actually acknowledged as Christians. This is
expressed, for example with the outpouring of the Spirit upon
them (8:17). The only problem is what capacity the apostles
are functioning here. It is inconceivable that the Spirit is tied
to the apostolic office and therefore cannot be mediated by a
non-apostle such as Philip. The point must lie in the relationship among Israel—the Spirit—the Twelve apostles—Jerusalem. According to Luke 22:29f. and Acts 1:15ff. the Twelve
are directly related to Israel; they are the eschatological regents
of the people of God.[47] It is precisely because they are regents
that they remain in Jerusalem the whole time. This is the perspective in the first eight chapters of Acts in which we get a
pointed account of the Jewish orthodoxy of the first Christians.
Furthermore, according to Luke the Spirit belongs to the restored people of God, as is clear from Acts 2:17ff. For Luke
the Spirit is so naturally associated with Israel that when the
Spirit is also given to non-Israelites, it is emphasized as a
special and dramatic occurrence (Acts 10:45: "The gift of the
Holy Spirit had been poured out even on the Gentiles").

It should be evident that the apostles by their visit have sanctioned Samaria as belonging to the restored Israel. The Samaritans, who previously rejected Jesus because he was on his way to Jerusalem now bind themselves to Jerusalem by receiving those who come from Jerusalem. As the listing of missionary territories shows, the restored Israel is found in Galilee, Judea and Samaria (1:8; 8:1; 9:31). For the doubters in Luke's milieu the account of the apostles' own approval of Samaria must be decisive. This in turn reveals something about Luke's audience; they are people who have some acquaintance with the Samaritans, and have had some misgivings regarding the Christian mission among the Samaritans. For these Jewish Christians Luke shows how the apostles themselves brought the lost sheep of the house of Israel back to Israel to be part of the restored people of God.

Notes

[1] R. Bultmann, *The Gospel of John,* trans. G. R. Beasley-Murray (Philadelphia: Westminster Press, 1971) 179, claims that the church in the beginning was intensely involved with the problem of the relations between Jesus and Samaritans and between the disciples of Jesus and the Samaritans. The problem does not arise in Acts 8 because the Samaritan mission is taken for granted. Bultmann does not mention that Luke alone takes up the issue, while in Matthew only a vestige of the problem remains.

[2] On the Samaritan element in the Gospel of John: J. A. Bailey, *The Traditions Common to the Gospels of Luke and John* (NovTSup 7; Leiden: E. J. Brill, 1963); E. D. Freed, "Samaritan Influence in the Gospel of John," *CBQ* 30 (1968) 580-587; and "Did John write his Gospel partly to win Samaritan Converts?" *NovT* 12 (1970) 241-256.

[3] Bultmann, 179, claims that v. 9c is a later gloss, and that the opposition between Jews and Samaritans was known by the Gospel's first readers.

[4] Cf. K. L. Schmidt, *Der Rahmen der Geschichte Jesus* (Berlin: Trowitzsch, 1919) 165.

[5] Thus Bultmann, 179.

[6] For Jesus' understanding: J. Jeremias, *Samareia TDNT* 7, 92f.

[7] For Luke's understanding of mission see my essay, "The Divided People of God," Parts I and II.

[8] Bailey, 104, claims that the Samaritan material is pre-Lukan; concerning the Samaritan sources in Acts see A. Spiro, "Stephen's Samaritan Background," *The Acts of the Apostles,* J. Munck (AB 31; New York: Doubleday, 1967) 285-300; cf. H. Conzelmann, *The Theology of St. Luke,* trans. G. Buswell (New York: Harper & Row, 1961) 71: The Samaritan accounts in Luke 10 and 17 belong to the local Jerusalem tradition.

[9] O. Bauernfeind, *Die Apostelgeschichte* (Leipzig: Deichert, 1939) 124.

[10] According to Bultmann, *History of the Synoptic Tradition,* trans. J. Marsh (New York: Harper & Row, 1963) 25-26, this is not ancient tradition because the journey through Samaria is a Lukan construction. For a variation see: F. Schütz, *Der leidende Christus* (Stuttgart: Kohlhammer, 1969) 74; W. Grundmann, *Das Evangelium nach Lukas* (Berlin: Evangelische Verlagsanstalt, 1966) 201; A. Schlatter, *Das Evangelium des Lukas* (Stuttgart: Calwer Verlag, 1931) 269; Schmidt, 269.

[11] Thus already H. Halevy, "Sens et origin de la parabole evangelique dite du bon Samaritain," *REJ* 4 (1882) 249-255. See further: J. D. M. Derrett, "Law in the New Testament: Fresh Light on the Parable of the Good Samaritan," *NTS* 11 (1964) 22ff. He attempts to understand the parable from methods of rabbinic interpretation. Luke's interpretation of the account remains unexplained. At any rate the triad, priest—Levite—Samaritan, makes no sense if the Samaritan is regarded as a Gentile; but it does make sense if he is viewed as an unacceptable Jew, an individual from those despised, the sinners, within Israel. The Samaritan would then have the same status as the publican in Luke 18.

[12] It is obvious that the Samaritan in contrast to the priest and the Levite keeps the law and fulfills its highest demand, namely the deed of mercy, *poiēsas to eleos,* v. 37. The context of the parable is concern for proper understanding of the law, vv. 25ff. If the Samaritan is not a Gentile in Luke's eyes, the triad is more easily understood: Two law-abiding Jews are put to shame by a contemptible Jew. This accords with the theologically important statement in Luke 7:29: The publi-

cans justified God in contrast to the Pharisees and lawyers. This in turn concurs with the Lukan apology, in which the church in contrast to the synagogue keeps the law of Moses; see my essay, "The Law in Luke-Acts." Thus, the church which carries out a mission in Samaria, or more properly, which has carried out a mission in Samaria, has by so doing not fallen away from the law.

[13] See Jeremias, 92; for a different opinion see J. Montgomery, *The Samaritans* (Philadelphia: J. C. Winston, 1907) 160. Both deal with Jesus' relation to the Samaritans rather than with Luke's view of that relationship.

[14] Montgomery, 160. See the comments in Josephus, *Ant.* 18:22 about the Samaritans' admission to the Temple.

[15] "Missionary mandate" is actually an improper designation; according to Luke the mission does not derive from Jesus' command but from Scripture. It is God's mandate, as clearly seen in Luke 24:44-47; Acts 13:47 and 15:16ff.

[16] It is not perfectly clear how the expression *to ethnos tēs Samareias* is to be understood. It need not signify anything more than the population of Samaria, just as *laos* is used in Acts 18:10. However, judging by Luke's general use of *ethnos* it is reasonable to suppose that the word has a certain ethnic quality.

[17] Cf. for example, Conzelmann, *Theology,* where the interest in Samaria is reduced to the question of whether Jesus travelled through this territory or not; see below note 25.

[18] Cf. for example, M. S. Enslin, "Luke and the Samaritans," *HTR* 36 (1943) 281; Jeremias, 94; J. Bowman, *Samaritanische Probleme* (Stuttgart: Kohlhammer, 1967) 62; E. E. Ellis, *The Gospel of Luke* (London: Nelson, 1966) 209; F. Hahn, *Mission in the New Testament,* trans. F. Clarke (Naperville: A. R. Allenson, 1963) 132—although Hahn is somewhat vague about the status of the Samaritans (he is clearer on 62, n. 2); cf. also H. J. Cadbury, *The Making of Luke-Acts* (London: S.P.C.K., 1961) 257.

[19] One difficulty in understanding the Samaritans in the New Testament is that we cannot know with certainty how they were regarded by the Jews at the time of Jesus and the early church. It is clear that attitudes in late Judaism were shifting and extremely varied. According to one widespread view at this time, the Samaritans were Jews, cf. Montgomery, 163ff. Montgomery refers (164) to Justin's *Apology,* in which Justin sees the Samaritans as a part of Israel. As a Jewish

sect: Eusebius, *H. E.* IV, 22; Ephiphanius, *Haer.* I, 10; cf. Montgomery, 252; see also Bowman, 54. The remark in S. G. F. Brandon, *The Fall of Jerusalem* (London: S.P.C.K., 1951) 128, that the Samaritans' entrance into the Christian church must have upset all loyal Jews, is not necessarily correct. It appears that many commentators have based their view of the Samaritans on the absolute schism between Jews and Samaritans which occurs only in the post-Christian era.

[20] This does not mean that Acts 10-11 begins the account of the development of the Gentile mission. Chapters 10-11 present for Jewish Christian readers a theological view of mission, rather than a historical report of its progress.

[21] Luke endeavors to show the Jewish character of Stephen and the circle about him. Stephen's sermon is, of course, meant to repudiate the false accusation that he spoke against the law of Moses and the Temple (6:11, 13, 14). The refugees (8:1, 4; 11:19), are also described as Jewish Christians, faithful to the law and loyal to Israel.

[22] On 15:3 and the status of the Samaritans see K. Bornhäuser, *Studien zur Apostelgeschichte* (Gütersloh: Bertelsmann, 1934) 90, and Bowman, 75.

[23] See my essay, "The Law in Luke-Acts."

[24] See above n. 16.

[25] Conzelmann, 31; 40f.; 49.; 54. See also V. Taylor, *Behind the Third Gospel* (Oxford: Clarendon Press, 1926) 91, and E. Lohmeyer, *Galiläa und Jerusalem* (Göttingen: Vandenhoeck und Ruprecht, 1936) 42.

[26] Conzelmann, 68ff.

[27] *Ibid.*, 36.

[28] See Ellis, 209; concerning Luke's acquaintance with Palestine see A. von Harnack, *Die Apostelgeschichte* (BENT III; Leipzig: Hinrichs, 1908) 71-89.

[29] Luke 6:17ff. is a possible exception. However, within the framework of Lukan theology, it is more likely that this passage concerns Jews from the regions which are named. Luke is, of course, consciously aware of the Jewish diaspora (Acts 2:9ff. and all the synagogue scenes in the second part of the book).

[30] Grundmann, 155, claims that Luke at this point reproduces a composite narrative. In agreement with E. Hirsch, he thinks that these two narratives must have been conflated prior to Luke. The reason is

that here we find marked Jewish Christian features, while Luke's special material is otherwise characterized by a universalistic tendency. Grundmann's view is determined more by previous research than by careful attention to Luke's special material.

[31] Thus Grundmann, 155f.

[32] So also Conzelmann, 71.

[33] Cf. Schmidt, 267.

[34] Concerning the question of Jesus' relationship to the law of Moses, cf. my essay, "The Law in Luke-Acts," 138-140.

[35] The concern is with the direct rejection of the missionary preaching, not with the persecution of missionaries who are placed on the scene for various other reasons. Luke takes up the Jews' rejection for theological reasons. With the preaching of the apostles, Israel passes through a crisis, in which the restored Israel is separated from the unbelieving. This process is necessary in order that the Gentiles may participate in the salvation of Israel. Luke has no corresponding interest in the Gentile reaction to the Christian message—for obvious reasons. The Areopagus speech is no contradiction; it is neither a missionary sermon nor a mission situation.

[36] According to Montgomery, 163, the Samaritans here are separated not only from "Jewry" but also from the rest of the world.

[37] In reference to Galilee see Haenchen's commentary on the passage. The impression "travel narrative" is meant to give the readers about Jesus' geographical activity makes it dubious whether Samaria is also included.

[38] See Hahn, 62, n. 2: They are second-class Jews.

[39] For the theology of the "travel narrative" see Schütz, 70ff.: The journey is meant to illustrate Jesus' demand on Israel. In my opinion Schütz is more correct than Conzelmann who sees the "journey" as an expression of Jesus' consciousness of suffering.

[40] See Conzelmann, 35.

[41] Montgomery, 160: *allogenēs* is a weaker word than *allophylos*. The latter is used in Acts 10:28.

[42] See H. L. Strack—P. Billerbeck, *Kommentar zum Neuen Testament* (München: Bech, 1928) I, 538ff.

[43] Bailey's suggestion, 109, that Luke considers Jesus' contact with the Samaritans an anticipation of the church's mission among Samari-

tans is probably correct, but it does little to explain much of Luke's theology.

[44] The motif of the destitute and hardened Israel is already encountered in the first chapters of Luke's gospel, especially 1:51ff. There is reason to examine anew the sections regarding the rich and poor in light of Luke's understanding of Israel as a destitute people.

[45] For the exegesis of this verse see my essay, "The Divided People of God," 51-53.

[46] See the commentaries of Haenchen and Conzelmann on this passage.

[47] More details in my essay, "The Twelve on Israel's Thrones."

The Law in Luke-Acts

I

In 1872, Franz Overbeck wrote an essay on Justin Martyr and Luke's Acts of the Apostles, stating that the author of Acts was unprincipled when he dealt with the law.[1] On the one hand, Luke advocates justification by faith apart from the law (13:38f.); on the other, Jewish Christians are obliged to keep the law unabridged, while Gentile Christians have only modified freedom from the law. Like Justin, the author of Acts tolerates Jewish Christian adherence to the law, whereas he pretends to regard it as compulsory. Actually, Luke merely toys with the problem;[2] the question is of no concern to him.

No matter what we may think of Overbeck's views, at least he has shown that to unravel Luke's attitude toward the law is problematic, and he has demonstrated that the solution is to be sought in the Jewish Christianity of Luke's time. It seems to be common opinion among scholars that the problem of the law is of no concern to Luke, as is evident from the lack of exhaustive monographs and essays. This opinion is expressed by leading contemporary scholars. Ernst Haenchen asserts that the problem is only peripheral in Acts.[3] According to Hans

Conzelmann, the debate regarding the law is presented solely
by means of historical reflection; the conflict is not actual and
acute. The dispute within the church regarding the law is in
itself a matter of history and not an acute problem. The solution, namely, freedom from the law, is by Luke's time an accomplished fact. The law is given up in principle by the
church and replaced by the apostolic decree; the law was
nothing but an "epoch" within redemptive history.[4]

Such opinions and their presuppositions need to be criticized.
The inclination to deal with the question as if it concerned
only soteriology and ethics is another problem, which is beyond the scope of this investigation. On the surface, Luke's
record seems to be but an echo of earlier debates and conflicts;
Gentiles are saved without circumcision and adherence to the
law. This, however, presupposes that Luke in all essentials is
concerned with Gentile Christianity. But Overbeck and later
Harnack[5] have raised a question which deserves attention:
Does Luke deal with the acute problems within Jewish Christianity?

Jewish sources demonstrate that the Mosaic law relates not
only to salvation, but to Israel's "identity" as the people of
God. The conflicts within early Christianity about the law not
only centered on the question of salvation, but also concerned
the relationship to Israel and the "self-understanding" of the
church. To the author of Matthew's Gospel, the law is a chris-
tological and ecclesiological problem. Jesus is the divinely
authorized interpreter of the law;[6] the church, "which yields
the proper fruits of the kingdom," has as its distinctive sign
adherence to the law, whereas the Jews do not keep the law
and are responsible for the death of the messianic interpreter
of the law.[7] For John the problem is in all essentials christo-
logical. Moses and the law are witnesses to Christ; they represent what is provisional and predict "grace and truth by
Jesus Christ" (1:17; 5:45).[8]

Most scholars, however, take it for granted that Luke considers the church to be "the new Israel," the universal people of God; thus the law is a matter of history, belonging to the old people, now replaced by the church. We should be hesitant about stating that the "identity-problem" of the church was solved by the catchword "the new Israel" as early as the New Testament. And surely it is out of place to speak too hastily of a new Moses, a new lawgiver and a new law.[9] The New Testament differs in this respect from the apostolic fathers. The term "the new Israel" cannot be found in the New Testament. I do not question that the idea is present there, at least in germinal form, but not as a general opinion. And this idea can certainly not be found in Luke-Acts.

Finally, it is commonly held that the solution was an accomplished fact by the time of Luke. My question is, where and when was the conflict settled? We may hardly refer to Paul, because Luke under no circumstances advocates a Pauline solution.[10] Paul was not generally accepted as an authority, not even by Luke. Before the writing of Luke-Acts and the rest of the New Testament one problem was essentially solved —the salvation of the Gentiles without circumcision. We may say that the problem was solved *de facto,* not *de jure,* that is, the idea was not developed into a generally accepted theology. The problem of the law was not solved by the admission of the uncircumcised. The problem was more complicated than that.

To Matthew, writing about A.D. 80, the question is still acute. The Gospel of John deals with it in its own way, differently from Matthew. A long time after the admission of Gentiles had become an accomplished fact, the problems regarding the law remained theologically unresolved. That is, we find in the New Testament a series of different and divergent solutions: Matthew, John, Paul, the Letter to the Hebrews, James' letter, etc. And the discussion continues through the second and even into parts of the third century.[11]

We do not know when, where, and under what circumstances the first Gentiles became Christians. Perhaps it was the outcome of enthusiastic and ecstatic experiences within the church. But the different approaches within the New Testament disclose that action preceded theology. And we do know for certain that after the acceptance of Gentiles, Jewish Christians, who represented no theological uniformity, faced severe problems: what about Israel, what about the people of God and election, what about the law and the covenant, what about circumcision? Throughout the first century the problem of the law and the problem of Israel are intertwined, and no ecclesiastical authority existed before which the dispute could be brought for its final and binding solution. It is a mere fiction to regard Luke as representative of some sort of ecclesiastical "establishment." Like other New Testament writers he gives a peculiar and characteristic interpretation when he deals with the significance of the law.

An examination of Luke's terminology regarding the law offers a hint that Luke is not only echoing previous solutions. His terminology differs from other New Testament writers and from the apostolic fathers. Some examples:

1. Only Luke employs terms like *nomos kyriou,* "the law of the Lord" (God)[12] and "the law of the fathers" (Luke 2:23, 24, 39; Acts 22:3).[13]

2. No one but Luke refers to the Mosaic law as "the customs," *ta ethnē,* which Moses delivered to us" and similar expressions (Acts 6:14; 15:1; 21:21; 28:17).[14]

3. Only Luke talks about "Moses being preached" (Acts 15:21), and uses the word *paranomein* (23:5).[15]

4. The law is "the living words," *logia zōnta,* (Acts 7:38), once again, solely a Lukan phrase.[16]

5. The expression "to speak against Moses, the law," is present only in Luke's writings (Acts 6:11, 13, 14 [18:13]; 21:21, 28; 25:8 [10]; 28:17).

6. The expression "the law of Moses," *nomos Mōuseōs,* is used five times by Luke; in other New Testament writings three times [17] (Luke 2:22; 24:44; Acts 13:38; 15:5; 28:23).

7. The name "Moses," referring to the law, appears frequently in Luke-Acts, seldom in other writings (Luke 5:14; 16:29, 31; 24:27; Acts 6:11; 15:1, 21; 21:21).[18]

Only to some extent are we able to find parallels, and we find them in Hellenistic Jewish sources. It is more Jewish than biblical phraseology, from the Septuagint, Josephus, Philo, etc. The terminology is rather peculiar, and we may say that it is conservative and Jewish, and it partially reveals Luke's view.

For Luke the law remains the law given to Israel on Sinai, in the strict meaning of the word, the law of Israel. And Luke is concerned about the law because it is Israel's law. Certainly Moses is a prophet as well (Acts 3:22; 7:37), but he is primarily associated with the law.[19] It is significant that Luke is most concerned about the ritual and ceremonial aspects of the law. The law is to him not essentially the moral law, but the mark of distinction between Jews and non-Jews.[20] The law is the sign of Israel as the people of God, which is evident from Luke's overall perspective and from individual passages.

Paul is accused of being an apostate who has forsaken Moses. In order to disprove the accusations and demonstrate his complete faithfulness to the law, Paul takes a Nazirite vow (Acts 21:15-26).[21]

The heart of the law is circumcision (Acts 15:1, 5; 16:3); Luke never spiritualizes or reinterprets this as is done elsewhere in the New Testament,[22] nor does Acts 7:51 represent any reinterpretation.[23] Circumcision and keeping the law go together (Acts 15:1, 5).

The life of the primitive church at Jerusalem as depicted in the early chapters of Acts is determined by universal adherence to the law, which is especially evident from the Christians' allegiance to the temple. The connection between temple and law is demonstrated in Acts 6-7, as in the exordium to the Gospel (Luke 1-2). Peter's and the other Christians' adherence to the law is essentially their obligation to ritual purity and consequently to strict separation from the uncircumcised, something which is evident in the Cornelius story (Acts 10:13ff., 28; 11:3). Significantly, Cornelius himself keeps the law (Acts 10:2, 4, 22) but without the one necessary thing, circumcision.[24]

The same viewpoints prevail in the preface to the Gospel, Chapters 1-2, where Luke depicts in detail how all the ritual prescriptions in the law are performed by Jesus' parents (2:21, 22, 24, 39; cf. Jesus as an apprentice of the law, a rabbinic disciple in the temple, 2:41ff.).[25] It is mere coincidence or solely pious ornamentation that the alleged universalistic Gospel of Luke insists on a circumcised Messiah?

It is significant that Luke in his Gospel avoids any criticism of the law or parts of it by Jesus, a criticism understood as reinterpretation in Matthew and Mark. Specific sayings in the preface to the speech of Stephen provide the explanation. The Jews charge Stephen with blasphemous statements against Moses, the law, God and the temple. This is defined more precisely: "the customs from Moses," the law, will be altered (6:14). This heretical and anti-Israelitic notion is attributed to Jesus. According to the charge Jesus is responsible for the alleged alterations of the Mosaic law. For Luke these accusations are patently false, which among other things the speech of Stephen is intended to prove. Obviously the saying in Acts 6:14 with the combination of temple-saying and statement about the law refers back to the Gospel. Consequently, in Luke's Gospel, every criticism is missing. Jesus did not alter anything; the law is permanently valid. Not even tacitly does Luke stress the moral aspect, and the relation between ethics and law remains remarkably obscure.

We shall illustrate Luke's position on some points:

1. For Luke there is no summary of the law in the one central commandment of love that would serve as some sort of basic norm or essence of the law (cf. Matthew, Mark, and Paul).[26] Like the rabbis, Luke does not in principle raise one commandment above others.[27] In the rewriting of Mark 12:28-34, Luke's version differs significantly (10:25ff.). The point at issue is not a first or great commandment, but inheriting eternal life.[28] A lawyer, not Jesus, provides the proper answer. Luke does not speak of the "weightier matters of the law" (Matt. 23:23), but the law consists of giving tithes *and* care for justice and the love of God (11:37ff.). Accordingly, love is not conceived as far more than sacrifices (Mark 12:33).

2. In Luke's treatment of Mark's pericope on divorce (10:1-12), he avoids the obvious renunciation of Moses. For Luke, the ban on divorce is not traced back to any new interpretation of the law or the will of God by Jesus; it is not the sign of a higher righteousness. Moses did not write a commandment "for the hardness of your hearts." In its context, Luke 16:18 serves as evidence for the perpetual validity of the Mosaic law, no matter how this may be explained.[29]

3. The important section in Mark 7:1-23, dealing with ritual cleanliness, is missing in Luke. Perhaps it disappears as part of the "great omission." On the other hand, some sayings seem to disclose that Luke knew the Markan record (cf. 11:37ff.). In any case, Luke does not offer any criticism concerning the rejection of God's commandments "in order to maintain the

tradition of men" (Mark 7:8; Matt. 15:3ff.). Luke, on the contrary, asserts that the "customs from the fathers" are in harmony with the law (Acts 6:14; 21:21; 28:17, cf. 10:14ff.; 11:3, 8). The same is evident from the first chapters of Acts, that is, in the description of the Christians' Jewish manner of life.

4. When Luke deals with the question of the cleansing of cups and plates (cf. Matt. 23:25f.), a seemingly enigmatic and awkward saying has caused scholars to suspect a mistranslation of the Aramaic "Give for alms what is in the cup, and all is clean" (11:41).[30] In my opinion this rewriting is done deliberately in order to give the saying a Jewish flavor. Almsgiving is important for Luke, and only for him among the New Testament writers, as a sign of true adherence to the law (11:41; 12:33; Acts 9:36; 10:2, 4, 31; 24:17).[31] Jesus' teaching is in accordance with the law.

5. There is no conflict with the law in Jesus' attitude as described in many disputes about the Sabbath. Luke records no less than four disputes,[32] and he is concerned to show that Jesus acted in complete accordance with the law, and that the Jewish leaders were not able to raise any objections. His idea is neither that "the sabbath was made for man" nor essentially that the saving of life allows for a transgression of the command. His principle may be found in Luke 13:10-17: It is no transgression to free a daughter of Abraham, an Israelite, on the Sabbath.[33] On the contrary, this is what the law demands.[34]

The law is of a divine nature, even delivered by angels (Acts 7:53). It consists of "living words" that are eternally valid (Acts 7:38; Luke 16:16f.).[35] Luke treats his traditions so that Jesus' adherence to the law and his faithfulness to the law since childhood are expressed. With Acts in mind, the reason for this is self-evident. Luke could not possibly depict the Christians at Jerusalem as "myriads of Jews, all zealous for the law" (Acts 21:21),[36] if he had described Jesus as altering, summarizing or reinterpreting the law.

Luke has the most conservative outlook within the New Testament,[37] because of his concern for the law as Israel's law, the sign of God's people. Luke has not consciously tried to Christianize the law or to interpret it with a view to the Christian church. This does not allow us to jump to the conclusion that Luke takes no interest in the whole problem. Repeatedly Luke refers to Jews' charging Christians with apostasy, with having abandoned the law. The sayings are worded by Luke himself, and they show the indissoluble connection between Israel and the law. The sayings are stereotyped; they have in all essentials the same content, and may safely be classified as formulas. They stand without parallels in Jewish and New Testament literature. The charges include apostasy and blasphemy against Moses, the law, Israel, and sometimes the temple (6:11, 13, 14; [18:13]; 21:21, 28; 25:8. [10]; 28:17). We find "sin against the law" and "sin against the people" linked together. To speak against the law is to propagandize against Israel as the people of God, and this sin refers primarily to the ritual aspect (21:21ff., 28ff.), that is, the law is conceived as *character indelebilis* of Israel. The sayings even show that Luke takes an interest in the law as a distinct entity and phenomenon, not as single commandments.

Now the question arises why this conservative outlook is so important to Luke. Why do Jewish Christians at Jerusalem and in the diaspora keep the law and so demonstrate its permanent validity? The answer is a fairly simple one. Luke knows only one Israel, one people of God, one covenant. He stresses repeatedly that the promises are given to Israel. This is emphasized in the exordium to the Gospel, which ought not to be neglected by redaction critics (1:16, 30ff., 54-59, 69-75; 2:10f, 32-33 etc.). It is reiterated in the speeches in Acts (1:8; 2:36, 39; 3:25f.; 13:26, 32f., etc.).

Further, the divine epithets in Acts are of a distinctively Jewish character. God is "the God of our fathers" (3:13; 5:30; 7:32; 22:14; 24:14); he is the "God of Israel," (Luke 1:68; Acts 13:17), or "the God of this people," (Acts 13:17); he is the "God of Abraham, Isaac and Jacob," (Acts 3:13; 7:32), or "the God of Jacob," (Acts 7:46).

As N. A. Dahl has demonstrated, the figure of Abraham is never Christianized in Luke-Acts;[38] Gentiles are not the sons of Abraham, and Abraham is not the father of uncircumcised Christians, but father of the circumcised. The promises belong to Abraham and his children (Luke 1:68-75; Acts 3:25f.; 7:1, 8).

It is of vital importance that the covenant given to Abraham is the covenant of circumcision (Acts 7:8), which at the same time involves Gentile participation in the promises to Israel (Acts 3:25f.; 15:16f.).[39] Circumcision and the succession of the circumcised warrant salvation (see Acts 7:6-7 compared with v. 8; this provides the link with the history of Abraham). Outside Israel, no salvation!

If we take these and corresponding sayings seriously, we may easily understand why Luke attaches importance to the Mosaic law and to the primitive church and Jewish Christians as being zealous for the law. Precisely in this manner they prove their identity as the people of God, entitled to salvation. The mark of distinction between Christian Jews and other Jews is not law or circumcision. The mark of distinction is that the Christian Jews believe *all things* in the law and the prophets, which includes the acceptance of the circumcised Messiah promised the people and now come.[40] Those who reject Jesus as the Messiah are extirpated from Israel; they have lost their inheritance.[41] Because Jewish Christians are the restored Israel,[42] circumcision and law become the very marks of their identity. According to Luke, a considerable number of pious Jews have become Christians, which is evident from the repeated mention of mass conversions among Jews.[43]

Thus one conclusion can be drawn: Luke's view of the law is bound up with his ecclesiology; it is a sign of the identity of the church. This is far more than Overbeck assumed, namely, that Luke could at least tolerate the Jewish Christians' adherence to the law,[44] Jewish Christians, being the restored Israel, are the foundation of the church, and so they must be upholders of the law. For Luke, salvation of Gentiles is beyond question, and they are saved as Gentiles (Acts 10-11 and 15). Luke accords with the common Christian view and follows general practice within the church. But the arguments he offers are peculiar to him.

The covenant of circumcision and the promises to Israel involve the Gentiles' participation in Israel's salvation (Acts 3:25; 15:14-17; Luke 2:46-47; Acts 13:47).[45] The people of the circumcision and the law will be saved, and "a people from the Gentiles" will join Israel (Acts 15:14).[46] The idea is that of a people and an associate people.[47] More important to us is the argument offered in connection with the apostolic decree. Luke labors to prove that the salvation of Gentiles occurs in complete accordance with the law; no transgression has taken place; the law is not invalidated, abridged or outmoded. The very image in Acts of the Jewish Christian church faithful to the law witnesses that the apostolic decree is neither an abrogation nor any new interpretation of the law. The authority of the decree is not due to its apostolicity; rather, according to Luke, it stems from James, the adherent of the law par excellence.[48] Scriptural proofs from the prophets ratify the admittance of Gentiles into the church (Acts 15:15ff.).[49]

Luke's general line of argument, however, is determined throughout by his appeal to the law *and* the prophets, and in this case the actual proof comes from Moses, the law. No matter how the complicated passage Acts 15:21 is to be interpreted in detail, the function of the verse is to validate the decree, to call upon Moses as witness. Everyone who truly hears Moses knows that the decree expresses what Moses demands from Gentiles in order that they may live among Israelites (15:15-17). The four prescriptions are what the law demands of Gentiles; perhaps Luke consciously refers to what Lev. 17-18 demands from the "strangers" that sojourn among Israelites.[50]

Once again Luke's choice of words is instructive. Luke employs such terms as *phylassein, diaterein* (15:29; 16:4; 21:25); these are technical terms in the Septuagint and the New Testament that refer to keeping the law.[51] Commentaries speak of the Gentiles' liberation from the law. This is not the whole truth. Luke knows of no Gentile mission that is free from the law. He knows about a Gentile mission without circumcision, not without the law. The apostolic decree enjoins Gentiles to keep the law, and they keep that part of the law required for them to live together with Jews. It is not lawful to impose upon Gentiles more than Moses himself demanded. It is false to speak of the Gentiles as free from the law. The church, on the contrary, delivers the law to the Gentiles as Gentiles. Thus Luke succeeds in showing complete adherence to the law as well as the salvation of Gentiles as Gentiles.

Luke does not champion any justification by law.[52] He may be both vague and indistinct in his soteriology. Nevertheless he expresses clearly that faith and conversion are God's work; it is by the grace of Jesus that Jews and Gentiles are saved (Luke 24:47; Acts 2:38; 3:19f.; 4:12; 13:39; 15:11; etc.). He employs Pauline usage, justification by faith in Acts 13:39. But this is never contrasted with adherence to the law; otherwise, he would have jeopardized his ecclesiology.

Conzelmann asserts that the law is replaced by the apostolic decree; the law belonged to the old Israel[53] and to the initial period of the church. I find this view unacceptable. According to Luke the church did not keep the law only until the Apostolic Council. After that meeting not only Paul but all other Jewish Christians observed the law, so that Paul immediately after the council circumcised one of his fellow workers (16:3; 21:15-26; 22-26). For Luke it is impossible that the law should be abrogated, replaced, or conceived as an epoch. This is apparent from the previously mentioned Jewish charges that the Christian Jews in the diaspora are taught by Paul to abandon circumcision and law. If Luke had championed the idea that the law was but provisionally valid, an epoch, he would have proved that the Jewish accusations were valid. But that is precisely what he tries to disprove.

We will take a closer look at these charges in order to clarify the situation and context of Luke's concept of the law. The charges and corresponding declarations of innocence are found no less than eight times (6:11, 13, 14; [18:13]; 21:21, 28; 25:8; 28:17). With the exception of 21:21 the charges come from non-Christian Jews. They are related to three persons, Jesus, Stephen, and Paul. Luke deals with the law essentially in connection with charges and declarations of innocence. His aims are apologetic. The charges come not from Christians (exception 21:21), but from outside the church. This indicates that Luke's main concern is not a problem within the church, but the conflict between church and synagogue. Luke's problem is not the influx of uncircumcised believers; he defends the rights of the uncircumcised within the scope of a more acute problem and crisis.[54]

The charges are that Stephen and Jesus alter the "customs from Moses," amend the law (6:11-14), that Paul invalidates the law, preaches apostasy from Moses, and thus speaks against Israel to Christian Jews (21:21, 28; 28:17). The point at issue is, according to Acts 21:21, the ritual prescriptions in the law, especially circumcision. Gentile Christians are not accused, and the charges have nothing to do with the apostolic decree, but refer to instructions allegedly given to Jewish Christians. Luke gives essentially one answer. He rejects the accusations as false and baseless, and he points as evidence to the complete faithfulness to the law that determines the life of the church. At the same time he charges the Jews with not keeping the law and rejecting Moses (Acts 7:35, 39, 53; 23:3 etc.). Luke does not say that the Jews have misunderstood the law, and there is no mention of a Jewish desire to be justified by the law.

To be sure, we do find some critical remarks (13:38; 15:10);[55] they are, however, but reminiscences and echoes from tradition and never developed into a theological concept. He never answers by giving a criticism of the law or any limitation of it determined by "salvation history." His answer is simply the complete faithfulness of Jewish Christians to the law (21:15ff.; 22; 23; 26). It is significant that the problems are related to Stephen and Paul. Luke also knows that Jesus was charged with abrogating the law. This indicates that Luke was aware of critical voices within the church that raised severe problems he had to face. In his Gospel and in Acts 6-7, he shows that Jesus did not criticize the law or object to it.

Paul is Luke's real problem. This is evident from Acts 21-28, chapters dedicated to Paul and the law.[56] Luke depicted Paul as the great missionary among Jews, who in every synagogue in the diaspora gathered the penitent Israel and taught them to adhere to circumcision and the law. And in the concluding chapters of Acts Paul is still the pious Pharisee faithful to the law.

Taking all these things into consideration, we should be able to detect the situation in which Luke's view was developed. He opposes Jews who charge Christian Jews with apostasy from Israel, which would mean that these Christian Jews would not be entitled to salvation.[57] And this conflict is related to Paul, who is used as an argument against the church. Paul himself indicates (Rom. 9-11) that he must reply to accusations of apostasy. At the time Luke writes the salvation of Gentiles creates no problem; this had been settled long ago. But the question about the law and Israel is still acute, because the Jewish element within the church is still a decisive factor, if not numerically at least theologically.

Luke's own position is independent and characteristic. By insisting on Jewish Christians' universal adherence to the law, he succeeds in showing that they are the restored and true Israel entitled to God's promises and to salvation. Overbeck asserted that Luke was unprincipled. This view is no longer tenable. It is correct to say that Luke intended to show that the Jewish Christians' observance of the law and the salvation of the Gentiles as an associate people, are the distinguishing marks of the Israel that Moses and the prophets predicted as the people of the promises of salvation.

Notes

[1] F. Overbeck, "Über das Verhältnis Justins des Märtyrers zur Apostelgeschichte," ZWT 15 (1872) 321ff.

[2] Cf. W. M. L. de Wette, *Kurze Erklärung der Apostlegeschichte* (4th ed. thoroughly revised and expanded by F. Overbeck; Leipzig: 1870) xxxff.: The Jewish element in Acts is not the attempt of the author to put himself in the position of an earlier Jewish Christianity, but is part of the Gentile Christianity Luke represents. The Christianity of Acts is, however, influenced by Judaism.

[3] E. Haenchen, *The Acts of the Apostles,* trans. B. Noble *et. al.* (Philadelphia: Westminster Press, 1971) 115f. and 223. See also F. J. Foakes-Jackson and Kirsopp Lake, *The Beginnings of Christianity* V (London: Macmillan, 1933) 217.

[4] H. Conzelmann, *The Theology of St. Luke,* trans. G. Buswell (New York: Harper and Row, 1961), 145ff. and 212f. Cf. Haenchen, 100. G. Bornkamm, G. Barth, H. Held, *Tradition and Interpretation in Matthew,* trans. P. Scott (Philadelphia: Westminster Press, 1963) 63.

[5] A. von Harnack, *Die Apostelgeschichte* (BENT III, Leipzig: Hinrichs, 1908) 208ff.

[6] Barth, 125-159.

[7] N. A. Dahl, "Die Passionsgeschichte bei Matthäus," *NTS* 2 (1955) 24ff.

[8] N. A. Dahl, "The Johannine Church and History," *Current Issues in New Testament Interpretation* (New York: Harper and Row, 1962) 130ff.

[9] The rabbinic notion of a "new law" is neither that of a completely new code to substitute for the Mosaic Torah, nor simply a new interpretation of the law, but above all an addition of new halakoth, which God himself formulates in heaven and which are not yet revealed to Israel—an idea to which most of the rabbis strongly objected. Cf. my essay "Die offenbarte und die verborgene Tora," *ST* 25 (1971) 90-108.

[10] P. Vielhauer, "On the 'Paulinism' of Acts," *Studies in Luke-Acts,* ed. L. E. Keck and J. L. Martyn (Nashville: Abingdon Press, 1966) 33-50.

[11] Cf. my article, "Ein Interpolator Interpretiert," *Studien zu den Testamenten der zwölf Patriarchen,* ed. W. Eltester (BZNW 36; Berlin: A. Töpelmann, 1969).

[12] LXX Exod. 13:9; 2 Kings 2:3; 1 Chron. 16:40; 2 Chron. 17:9; 25:4; 31:3; 34:14; 35:26; 1 Esd. 1:33; 8:7ff.; 9:48; etc. A similar expression is found in Barn. 2:6 but there the "Lord" is Jesus.

[13] 2 Macc. 6:1 (cf. v. 6); 7:2; 3 Macc. 1:23; 4 Macc. 9:1; 16:16; *Ant.,* 13:54.

[14] 2 Macc. 11:25 *(progonon);* 4 Macc. 18:5; *JW* 7.424; cf. also Philo, *de praem.* 106; *de spec. leg.* II, 148; *de somn.* II, 78; *vit. mos.* I, 31; II, 193; etc.

[15] LXX Job 34:18; Psa. 25:4; 70:4; 74:4; 118:51; 4 Macc. 5:17, 20, 27; 8:14; *JW* 2, 317; *Ant.* 11, 49.

[16] As far as I can see, there are no exact verbal parallels in Hellenistic Jewish literature.

[17] John 7:23; 1 Cor. 9:9; Heb. 10:28.

[18] When the name "Moses" is used in conjunction with the law, the reference is usually to single commandments. Mark 1:44; 10:3-4; 7:10; Matt. 8:4; 19:7 but note 22:24. Cf. also John 5:45f.; 7:22; 2 Cor. 3:15; Heb. 7:14.

[19] N. A. Dahl, "The Story of Abraham in Luke-Acts," in *Studies in Luke-Acts*, 139. Cf. also Conzelmann, 166f.

[20] An opposing view: Conzelmann, 92. According to T. Holtz, *Untersuchungen über die alttestamentlichen Zitate bei Lukas* (TU 104; Berlin: 1968) 171, Luke is not familiar with the nomistic trends in Judaism. See, however, Holtz's treatment of Acts 7, on 109ff.: The fundamental component of Stephen's speech is Jewish and "unthinkable for a Christian."

[21] On the figure of Paul in Acts, cf. Vielhauer, 33-50; my essay, "Paul: The Teacher of Israel."

[22] Rom. 2:29; Phil. 3:3: Col. 2:11.

[23] The idea is not to devaluate circumcision as if it were of no significance, but to stress the misbehavior of the Jews: They act as if they were not circumcised.

[24] Luke takes pains to demonstrate that Peter's visit to Cornelius does not imply any transgression of the law. He is aware that it is unlawful for a Jew "to associate with or to visit anyone of another nation" (10:28; 11:3). The problem in Chapters 10-11 is not the Gentile mission as such, as 11:1 shows. The church at Jerusalem does not object to Gentiles' receiving the gospel; that is taken for granted (Luke 24:47ff. and Acts 1:8). But they criticize Peter because he has kept company and eaten with uncircumcised men. Luke solves the problem by showing on the one hand that by means of visions, God himself compelled Peter to go to Cornelius; and on the other hand, that the Gentiles have now (!) become cleansed (10:15, 28; 11:8; 15:9). Thus Peter has not transgressed the law, for when Peter entered his house, Cornelius was "clean"; further support is provided by the demonstration of Cornelius' "Jewishness" (10:2, 4, 22).

[25] For Luke the Temple is not only the proper place for worship, but it is especially the place for teaching the law.

[26] Matt. 7:12; 22:24-30; Mark 12:28ff.; Rom. 13:8ff.; Gal. 5:14. It is however, questionable whether Matthew intended to elevate one commandment above the others (cf. 5:17ff.; 23:3); his idea is obviously that none of the commandments should be neglected.

[27] Even if the rabbis occasionally recognize a summary of the law in one or a few central commandments, this has no fundamental significance, because in principle each commandment is as important as the rest. Cf. Str.-B I, 907ff.; Gutbrod's article on *nomos* in *TDNT* IV, 1059; I. Abrahams, *Studies in Pharisaism and the Gospels I* (Cambridge: Cambridge University Press, 1917) 24ff.; Barth, 77f.

[28] Only Luke among the Gospel authors quotes Lev. 18:5: *touto poiei kai zēsē*—and without any critical note. Cf. Rom. 10:5; Gal. 3:12.

[29] The Lazarus story serves as proof for the continuing validity of every dot of the law. The rich man does not obey "Moses and the prophets" (16:29, 31); he transgresses the law by his lack of deeds of charity. Lazarus is not only a poor man, but a poor Israelite (v. 22f.), just as the rich man is depicted as an Israelite (vv. 24ff.). So Jesus' teaching on "God and mammon" is an interpretation of the law, which the Pharisees, "who were lovers of money" (v. 14) are not able to understand.

[30] M. Black, *An Aramaic Approach to the Gospels and Acts* (3rd ed.; Oxford: Clarendon Press, 1967) 2.

[31]Almsgiving is primarily conceived as a duty to Israel as the people of God (Acts 10:2; 24:17). In this context Luke treats one of his favorite topics, poverty and riches, which has been overlooked by redaction critics. The theme of aiding the poor within Israel appears in the preface (1:51ff.) as well as in the rest of the Gospel (chapters 12 and 16 in particular).

[32] 6:1-5, 6-11; 13:10-17 and 14:1-6.

[33] E. Haenchen characterizes v. 16 as a Jewish Christian reminiscence: *Der Weg Jesu* (Berlin: Töpelmann, 1966) 127f. But this alleged reminiscense fits too neatly with all other sayings of Jewish flavor in Luke-Acts and cannot be dismissed as an insignificant vestige.

[34] Cf. John 7:22f.

[35] The statement, "the law and the prophets were until John" obviously does not mean that the law and the prophets were but an "epoch" —see v. 17! The verse means that only since John is the kingdom preached.

[36] Cf. E. Haenchen, *Acts,* 608, on the problems connected with this verse.

[37] See Harnack, 212ff.

[38] "The Story of Abraham in Luke-Acts," 139ff.

[39] See my article "The Divided People of God," Part IV.

[40] Cf. Acts 24:14; 3:18, 24; 10:43; Luke 18:31; 24:25, 27, 45; further, Luke 13:28; 11:49f.; Acts 7:52. Luke stresses a) *all things* which are written, and b) *all* the prophets as witnesses to Jesus.

[41] Esp. Acts 3:25f.

[42] Cf. my essays, "The Divided People of God: The Restoration of Israel and Salvation for the Gentiles," and "Paul: The Teacher of Israel."

[43] On the significance of the mass conversions see my essay, "The Divided People of God," Part II.

[44] Overbeck's view more closely approximates Paul's attitude towards Jewish Christians, 1 Cor. 9:19ff.

[45] For an exegesis of Acts 13:47, see "The Divided People of God," 60 f.

[46] Dahl, "A People for His Name," *NTS* 4 (1957) 319-327.

[47] Cf. Harnack, 215.

[48] Cf. my essay, "James: The Defender of Paul," 190-193.

[49] On this passage, see "The Divided People of God," 51-53.

[50] Cf. H. Waitz, "Das problem des sogenannten Aposteldekrets," *ZKG* 55 (1936) 277.

[51] According to Harnack, 213, Luke sees in the law a saving effect, that is, for Christian Jews.

[52] See my essay, "James: The Defender of Paul."

[53] See above, note 4.

[54] On the following, cf. "Paul: The Teacher of Israel," Parts III and IV.

[55] The idea is obviously not that it is in principle impossible to keep the law, which would make all other Lukan statements inconceivable, but that we, that is, Jews and Christian Jews, have so far not kept the law, something which the history of Israel demonstrates (Acts 7:53).

[56] See my analysis in "Paul: The Teacher of Israel."

[57] Harnack, 214. Luke's way of dealing with the problem of the law reflects a historical situation in which Jewish Christians are an influential segment of the church.

Paul: The Teacher of Israel

The Apologetic
Speeches of
Paul in Acts

I

The speeches in Acts have given rise to numerous investigations. Whenever we refer to the speeches in Acts without further qualification, we usually mean the missionary speeches in Chapters 1-17. It is primarily on this basis that the attempt has been made to portray Luke as a "historian" and as a writer with theological concerns. The apologetic speeches of Paul have received only second-rate treatment. This is all the more remarkable since in the last part of Acts, Chapters 21-28, there are no less than four speeches or fragments of speeches of this type (22:1-21, 23:1ff., 24:10-21, and 26:1-23). These speeches differ in form and content from the rest of the speeches in Acts and do not fit into the pattern of the missionary speeches. Fifty per cent of Paul's speeches in Acts are of an apologetic type.

The entire section 21-28 is devoted to the defense of Paul. Luke grants as much space to Paul's trial as to his whole missionary activity. This indicates unambiguously that Luke's description of Paul in Acts is intended as a defense of the apostle. When Luke writes about Paul as a missionary with

153

special status in the church and in history,[1] he does it not to *describe* Paul's missionary activity, but to *explain* and *defend* it.[2] Martin Dibelius is scarcely correct when he maintains that Luke had only a meager tradition at his disposal.[3] But he is no doubt correct that it is in the speeches that Luke's views are expressed, namely in the choice and arrangement of material. Our question is what Luke intends with the speeches in Chapters 22-26 and how they are to be understood in relation to the preceding portions of Acts.

With regard to these concluding chapters, Dibelius maintains that Luke accords so much space to the trial of Paul because he wants to aid and support persecuted Christians.[4] Scholars who otherwise side with Dibelius have not followed him at this point.[5] There is therefore little reason to begin my own proposal by taking issue with this particular view of Dibelius. Yet the scholars concerned have attached little weight to the significance of that factor which both renders the view of Dibelius impossible and which can also lead to a fundamentally more correct understanding.

This factor is the biographical character of the speeches, to which nothing corresponds in the rest of the speeches in Acts. It is only in connection with Paul that the biographical element was necessary. We will have ample opportunity to return to this later. But this much by way of anticipation; what is said in these speeches is appropriate to Paul alone, as Luke views him. Luke knows no other person in the church who is in a corresponding situation and requires the same defense. Least of all could Paul, as the last Pharisee and the first missionary to the diaspora, serve as an example in a church that is primarily Gentile Christian—and according to common opinion, Luke's is a Gentile Christian church.

The traditional and still predominant understanding of these speeches also fails to do justice to the peculiar concentration on the person of Paul. According to this view, it could as well have been Peter or James who appeared in court; the concern in the trial chapters is for the church or Christianity and not the person of Paul. According to common opinion, the speeches represent political apologetic, with Rome, Caesar and the state as addressees. To put it more concretely, in this portion of Acts, with its marked political character, Luke has in view politically influential heathen in the Roman Empire.[6] That Acts would accordingly be addressed to a double readership—Christians, who are to be edified, and heathen, who are to be influenced politically—is something which we can leave out of consideration. This political-apologetic aspect, which is found already in Overbeck,[7] appears in numerous variations. It is most commonly bound up with the problem of *religio licita*.[8] What is at stake is the preservation of Christianity within the bounds of Judaism in order to procure peace and the opportunity to practice religion within the framework of the political recognition accorded Judaism. Hans Conzelmann calls into question the concept *religio licita* in this context and asserts that Luke is appealing to the state's ability to make reasonable judgments. Jewish-Christian belief in the resurrection lies outside its sphere of authority.[9] But with Conzelmann as well the political apologetic is predominant.

It is nevertheless evident that the attempt to fit the total content of the trial chapters into this framework meets with difficulties. Thus we encounter various subsidiary motifs which are connected to the main theme that Luke wants to justify the Gentile mission once again in Acts[10] and to demonstrate its legitimation in the Damascus experience of Paul.[11] He wants to portray Paul's exemplary confidence in the face of "principalities and powers," namely, Caesar and the Empire.[12] Here it appears difficult to maintain that the concern is for the good-will and protection of the state. Further: Luke wants to render an account of the relationship between Christianity and Judaism,[13] or Christianity, Judaism and the Roman State.[14]

We must to a certain extent dwell on the question of political apologetic. W. G. Kümmel, a reasonable and eminent scholar, maintains in his comprehensive introduction that we cannot overlook a certain defense against charges that the church is hostile to the state. Yet in a missionary writing directed to Gentiles, as Acts is, this is a secondary concern.[15] Kümmel's view may be correct. But first there are two questions to be answered:

1. To what extent is the political defense connected with Luke's sources and tradition? Here we encounter the difficult and somewhat neglected question of tradition and redaction in Acts.

2. How can the political-apologetic outlook be understood within Acts as a whole and within the theology Luke develops elsewhere? Thus, what sort of connection exists between Chapters 22ff. and the preceding portions of Acts? If the speeches of Paul are to be understood as political apologetic, then this portion of Acts is left hanging in the air and appears as an appendage.[16] The possibility is of course not thereby excluded that politics may be a concern.

We will not answer the question we have posed directly, but by means of the interpretation presented in what follows. Nevertheless, some factors should be expressed here which must raise suspicions about Luke's alleged political concern.

C. K. Barrett correctly maintains that the theological argumentation of the speeches is unintelligible to the Roman authorities.[17] We may add that Luke expresses this clearly by having the governor Festus request the Jewish King Agrippa for help in order to gain even the slightest notion about what is going on (25:24-26:3). The fact that the state and the Roman

Empire are never dealt with in principle is an issue in itself.[18] But more important is the portrayal of Roman officials which Luke presents in Chapters 22ff. According to common opinion, Luke describes the Romans as well-disposed toward the church. It is clear, however, that the Roman officials frequently appear in a somewhat unfortunate light in Luke's work [19]—a curious way of proceeding *vis a vis* the court whose understanding or protection is being sought.

The two main Roman characters, the governors Felix and Festus, are pro-Jewish and seek to decide the matter in favor of the Jews and against Paul. Festus wants to transfer the trial to Jerusalem. By means of Paul's words, Luke characterizes this proposal as an attempt to hand Paul over to the Jews for the sake of political profit (25:9-11). To obtain personal gain from the Jews, Felix leaves Paul in prison, against his better judgment and contrary to the law (24:27). Felix, who is married to a Jew and who according to Luke knows Christianity well (24:22), is downright corrupt (24:26). Only Paul's Roman citizenship and his appeal to Caesar save him from the Jewish plots against his life as well as from the greed and political maneuvering of the Roman officials, since with the appeal the affair is taken out of the hands of the provincial officials (23:27, 22:25ff., 25:9ff.).[20] It hardly appears as though Luke reckons with a favorable outcome of the trial!

If we are to speak at all of a general view of heathen authority and the Roman State, it seems obvious to point out that in 4:27 Pilate is described as Jesus' murderer. It may be said that here we are dealing with tradition. In that case one may ask whether Luke would make use of such a tradition if it were his intention to make a favorable impression on the Roman authorities. Finally, Luke's conception of God, who governs history by means of miracles and mighty deeds and delivers apostles from all prisons and perils, makes it difficult to imagine that it is Luke's desire to petition the Romans for favorable conditions and the opportunity to practice religion for the church.[21]

II

We now turn to the more positive side and examine the place of the trial chapters in the composition of Acts and the relationship between these chapters and the most important views Luke has expressed elsewhere. Since the position advocated here differs from common views, it should be set forth in detail. Acts can hardly be partitioned into clearly defined units, but the main train of thought may be sketched as follows:[22]

1. Luke has described the decisive turning point in the history of Israel[23] as the rise of a restored Israel consisting of repentant Jews, faithful to the law who believe in Jesus. The activity of the twelve apostles among the Jews has resulted in the conversion of half of Jerusalem (the reports of Jewish mass conversions)![24] Salvation belongs to the restored Israel, while the obdurate Jews are excluded from the people, salvation and history. This is accomplished principally in Chapters 1-8.

2. As a result of the renewal and restoration of Israel, the Gentiles receive a share in the salvation of God's people in accordance with the promises of God.[25] The mission among the Gentiles is instituted and acknowledged, and the problems within the church associated with it are solved. Rank and status of the Gentiles in the restored Israel are clarified.[26] On the basis of a special call to become a missionary to the diaspora and the Gentiles, Paul has carried out a mission in the diaspora of Asia Minor, with the result that a "people from the Gentiles" has become "associated" with Israel.[27] We encounter these views essentially in Chapters 9-15.

3. Luke has described the activity of Paul among the Jews

of the Greek diaspora, as a result of which numerous congregations of repentant Jews have arisen with which Gentiles have become associated. The mission among Jews proceeds toward its completion; only Rome remains (28:17ff.). As in Asia Minor, so in Greece the mission among Jews and Gentiles is traced back almost exclusively to Paul. And Luke emphasizes that Paul is at the point of concluding his work.

He has taken leave of the churches he has founded, represented by the Ephesians, and has left behind for them his testament (20:17ff.). According to Luke, Paul is now a figure well-known among Jews throughout the world.[28] Rumors concerning his teaching and preaching have reached the Jews in Jerusalem (21:20ff.). This leads to unrest among the tens of thousands of Christian Jews in Jerusalem who are zealous for the law, but the problems are solved by Paul's demonstration of his fidelity to the law (21:20ff.). We have thereby outlined the main ideas in Chapters 16-21.

The controversy concerning Paul's relationship to the law forms the direct prelude to the trial chapters and to the conclusion of Acts. From 21:27 to the end of the work, attention is focused on Paul and the Jews. What role is played by Rome and the state? The trial, which reaches a deadlock and is never decided, leads not to Caesar but to the Jews in Rome (28:17ff.). Apart from a few verses, Luke uses the whole account of Paul's stay in Rome to describe two meetings with the Jews. Luke states that the reason for the meeting with the Jewish leaders is that Paul wants to give an account of his relationship to Israel and the law in connection with the trial (28:20; cf. vv. 17-19). The Roman Christians, about whom Luke knows, do not appear on the scene; the government officials are only the "hosts" of the apostle (28:16, 30); and the Gentiles appear on the periphery (28:28), almost for the sole purpose of indicating how Acts will continue. It could be of course that Acts was written before the outcome of the trial was clear. But such an early date for the document encounters difficulties.[29] The assumption is more probable that the conclusion of the Acts of the Apostles now before us indicates that Luke has said everything he wanted to say.

It is accordingly not the intention of the trial chapters to present a historical account, but to supply the framework for Luke's real concern. If we consider 28:17ff. in relation to what precedes, it becomes clear that the literary function of the trial chapters consists in leading the apostle to Rome, yet not to Caesar but to the Roman Jews, where the final confrontation with the obdurate portion of Israel takes place. The trial fades into the background and the Romans disappear from the scene. Yet the trial, with its four speeches of Paul, is developed so extensively that it obviously cannot have been intended solely as a literary device to show how Paul reaches Rome and preaches in the world capital to Jews and Gentiles. The description has in this regard a clearly independent significance. The long drawn-out trial provides a broad framework which makes it possible to accommodate four speeches by Paul, by means of which Luke can complete his description of the apostle. In this way he can, among other things, introduce the Damascus event twice and thus describe it *in extenso*. It is clear that Chapters 22-26 form neither an appendage of a political-apologetic sort nor a transitional element that is to prepare for the conclusion. Luke's understanding of the church and his description of the apostle given earlier in Acts necessitate so extensive a defense of Paul.

Yet we do not want to anticipate but to go a bit deeper into the structure, style and character of the speeches. Luke himself emphasizes that these are apologetic speeches by using the words *apologeisthai* and *apologia* several times as catch-words in this context (22:1; 24:10; 25:8; 25:16; 26:1, 2, 24).[30] With regard to style and content, we have to do neither with missionary speeches nor with sermons. It is not the intention to carry on missionary work with these speeches.[31] Neither calls to repentance nor invitations to conversion are found here. There is no scriptural proof, no appeal to eyewitnesses. The well-established component in the missionary speeches intended for the Jews in Acts, the indictment on account of the murder of the Messiah, is lacking (2:23, 36; 3:14f., 27; 4:10; 5:30; 10:40; 13:27ff.). Neither is any kerygma to be found here. It appears to be present in one passage (26:23), but there it is not intended as preaching or proclamation but as an apology for the fact that Paul's preaching of Christ really consists only in what the law and the prophets say about the Messiah.

The speeches receive their character and their peculiar stamp from the role Paul plays in them. These speeches are appropriate to no one else and can be placed in the mouth of no one else. They are obviously spoken in the I-form, but we find here no representative or typical "I." This becomes clear from the strictly biographical character of the speeches, from which it may be gathered that what is said cannot be applied to others. Paul is neither type nor paradigm; he appears rather as an individual. The description of Paul as a Pharisee and a persecutor is unique; Paul's experience at Damascus and his missionary activity are peculiar to him. The object of the defense here is not Christianity or the individual Christian, but the person and activity of Paul.

It is not possible to speak of a unified composition or structure of the speeches. In this case as well they assume a position different from the missionary speeches. Yet it would appear that in two of the speeches Luke has made use of a pattern available to him. The pattern appears to be essentially as follows:

1. Description of Paul's life as an orthodox Jew, his education and training in Jerusalem, and his Pharisaism (22:3, 26:4-5).

2. Paul as persecutor of the Christian churches (22:4-5, 26:9-11). At both points Paul cites leading Jews as witnesses (22:5, 26:5).

3. The Damascus event (22:5-16, 26:12-18).

4. Paul's missionary commission, which is formulated quite differently in the two accounts (22:17-21; 26:16b-18). In Chapter 26 there is added to this a description of Paul's missionary activity (vv. 19ff.).

When we speak of a pattern in this case and of Luke's inability to arrange his material "freely," it is not based on the lack of correspondence between the Jewish charges and the content of the speeches (cf. 21:28 in comparison with 22:1ff.); the point is rather that the pattern can in the last analysis be traced back to Paul's own defense of his missionary activity and his apostleship in the face of Jews and Judaizers (cf. Phil. 3:3ff.;[32] Gal. 1:13ff.; compare also 1 Cor. 15:8f. and 2 Cor. 11:22).[33] It is impossible that Luke has formulated it on the basis of knowledge of the Pauline letters.

The material stems from Pauline tradition which has undergone its own history of transmission, which can be inferred from the inconsistencies in Luke's accounts in Chapters 9, 22 and 26. Nevertheless, the speeches in Chapters 22 and 26 are not quite sufficient to make clear what Luke is after in his apology for Paul. For this reason the speech fragment in Chapter 23 and the speech in Chapter 24 appear as supplement and interpretation. If the speeches in Chapters 22 and 26 are considered by themselves, they give the impression that Paul's Jewish orthodoxy and his Pharisaism belong to a past stage, a pre-Christian period in his life. Luke has more to say on this subject, however. The intervening speeches in 23 and 24 indicate that Paul is still a Pharisee (23:6); as a faithful son of his people he still serves the God of his fathers and believes the law and the prophets (24:14-16); his whole life up to his arrest in the temple is a demonstration of orthodox Jewish adherence to the law (24:17ff).[34]

The four speeches form a unity, and only when they are understood from the perspective of this inner unity can one recognize the picture Luke wants to paint. In Chapters 22 and 26 Luke clearly makes use of pre-formed material without making any alteration, while his commentary on the material is found in Chapters 23 and 24. From the way Luke interprets his material three factors in the speeches achieve decisive significance:

1. Paul was and is a Pharisee and a Jew who is faithful to the law (22:3; 23:1, 3, 5, 6; 24:14; 26:4-5).

2. He believes everything that is written in the law and the prophets, and he teaches only what Scripture says. Nothing in his preaching and teaching is un-Jewish (24:14f.; 26:22f).

3. He is charged because he preaches the resurrection, whereby it should be observed that the resurrection expresses God's promises to the people and the hope of Pharisaic Israel (23:6, 24:21, 26:6-8). Belief in the resurrection means fidelity to Scripture, law and people (24:14ff.; 26:22f).

III

These elements reveal what it is that Luke is concerned about in the apologetic speeches. Luke makes it clear that the church has levelled no accusations against Paul, and in 21:15-26 Luke deals conclusively with the final inner-church problem concerning Paul. The problem in 21:20ff. is the same, both for the Jewish Christians who are zealous for the law, and the Jews. The disquieting rumors which have reached the church are occasioned by Jewish accusations (21:21).

On several occasions Luke summarizes the charges directed against Paul in short formulas. In contrast to the speeches, in which Luke makes use of material that has been previously shaped, these summaries stem from Luke himself. They are of a uniform composition, homogeneous in content, and are inserted into the composition deliberately. Three of these summaries frame the portrayal of the trial as a whole:

1. 21:21 From the Jewish side it is reported that Paul teaches the Jews of the diaspora apostasy from Moses, that they should not circumcize their children, and that they do not need to live according to the customs of the fathers (the law).[35]

2. 21:28 Paul teaches everywhere against the people, the law and the temple.

3. 28:17 In Paul's declaration of innocence, he maintains that he has done nothing against the customs of the fathers (the law) and the people.

Added to this is a further declaration of Paul's innocence in 25:8; he has sinned neither against the law, the temple, nor Caesar. In 24:5 Tertullus asserts in his charge that Paul is creating dissensions[36] among Jews throughout the world and that he tried to profane the temple; finally he makes explicit reference to the concrete reason for the uproar in Jerusalem, 21:28b—something that disappears in the rest of the account of the trial. To the preceding we may add the Roman version of the Jewish charges. Claudius Lysias writes that the problem concerns disputes regarding "their [the Jews'] law," (23:29; cf. also 25:19).

By means of these summaries of charges and declarations of innocence, Luke makes it clear how he intends the description as a whole to be understood. This is expressed particularly in the framing of the portrayal as a whole; 21:21 and 28 state the theme to be dealt with in the speeches, and the conclusion is given in 28:17. Verses 25:8c and 24:5 indicate that Luke is clear about the historical framework and does not lose sight of it. Yet his concern is not to give a description of the trial for its own sake.

As to the content of the charges, three things are to be observed. First, the issue is what Paul is alleged to have taught Jews everywhere in the diaspora (21:21, 28;[37] cf. 24:5). As a consequence of the account Acts gives of Paul's missionary activity, he can here reflect on his work as a teacher in many parts of the world (*didaskein* in 21:21 and 28)! The problem has to do with Paul as the teacher of Israel.

According to the charges and rumors, Paul is a false teacher in Israel. The place which the charges occupy within the composition—after the account of Paul's world-encompassing missionary work—reveals how important it is for Luke to show that the issue here is not a "local debate" but a question that concerns Jews throughout the world. It must be emphasized that the charges, as Luke renders them, do not relate to the mission among the Gentiles.[38] It is often overlooked that the Jews described in Acts are not hostile toward the Gentiles, and they are not unwilling to allow them a share in salvation.[39] The degree to which Gentiles are to share in salvation is not problematic, but rather when and how it should be allotted them, that is, with or without circumcision and complete fulfillment of the law.[40]

Luke has already dealt with this problem in Chapters 10-11 and 15, and a final ecclesiastical ratification appears in 21:25. Further, just as the Gentile mission is not cited as the basis for the accusations against Paul, so also it does not appear as a theme in Paul's apologetic speeches. The main point is not what Paul teaches Gentiles, nor is it that he preaches to them; rather, it consists in what he teaches Jews and that he is precisely the one who appears as the teacher of Israel. Obviously 22:17-22 can be cited as a counter-argument. Paul is interrupted exactly at the point where he deals with his commission to the Gentiles, because Jerusalem (not Jews in general!) will not accept his preaching.[41] Yet this argument is too weak to justify the assertion that the Gentile mission forms the theme of 22-26 as a whole. First of all 26:17f., 19, 23, contradict 22:17-21. According to Chapter 22, Paul is not to preach in Jerusalem and before Jews; on the other hand, in Chapter 26 the preaching before Jews "from Jerusalem" is the main point, and the Gentile mission forms only an appendage to the mission to Jews.[42] It is difficult to understand how the inconsistencies are to be explained by appealing to Luke's intention in each case individually.[43] It is likewise inexplicable how Luke, if he wants to defend Paul's mission, can proceed with such carelessness that he contradicts in Chapter 26 what he wants to express in Chapter 22 and thereby in the apologetic speeches in general. Moreover 22:17-21 is not in keeping with Luke's total composition of Acts, where all preaching begins with the Jews.[44] Furthermore, the Gentile mission is not mentioned once in the speeches of Chapters 23 and 24 and likewise not in the summary in 28:17ff.

Acts 22:17-21 can only be explained by Luke's having before him various traditions regarding the story of Paul's conversion[45] that he does not want to "suppress;" and the inconsistencies in 22 and 26 show that here the Gentile mission is not what is of primary importance for Luke. However else the conversion story may be used, in this context at least it does not serve as a defense for the Gentile mission.

Let us return to the summaries of the charges. In the second place, it does not emerge from the charges that Paul is guilty of political rebellion. The speeches are not fashioned as an answer to such a charge. Luke emphasizes that the problem is not sedition by letting the Romans give their own version of the Jewish charges on several occasions. In Claudius Lysias' letter to Felix it is reported (23:26ff.) that Paul is accused only about questions of "their law" and that he is charged with nothing deserving death (v. 29).[46]

It is impossible that this verse be understood to imply that the Jews had made such a charge, but that it had been dismissed. That can be inferred from the relation of 29a to 29b. In 25:17-21, 26-27, Festus explains to Agrippa that he is unable to make the charges intelligible to Caesar. That is not because he has found Paul innocent, but because a charge of sedition is lacking. In v. 18, Festus expressly emphasizes that he expected such a charge, but instead the problem is about inner-Jewish differences of which he understands nothing (v. 19f.). The scene with Agrippa in 26:3 makes it clear that Luke wants to leave no doubt that the matter at issue is an affair which only a Jew can understand; that is, it is a debate within the people of God. It should therefore be clear that for Luke, in his account of the trial, the accusation of the orator Tertullus in 24:5—that Paul is the instigator of *staseis*—does not imply rebellion, but division, schism or dissension within world-wide Judaism.[47] It is therefore not the case that the Romans find the charges of sedition insupportable, but that according to Luke charges of this nature have not been made at all. Such charges are found in Acts 17:5, but Luke has taken great pains to keep them out of Chapters 22-26.

The manner in which Luke formulates the charges, the content of the speeches, and the statements of the Romans should be sufficient to show that it is not Luke's intention to explain Paul's personal political innocence nor that of the church in general. The biographical character of the speeches makes the latter impossible. Acts 25:8c is an insufficient basis for making a contrary assertion. Luke is occupied with another problem, which leads us back once again to the summaries of the charges.

In the third place, it emerges from the charges relating to Paul's teaching among the Jews of the diaspora that he teaches against people, law and temple (21:28). In 28:17, it is repeated: Paul has done nothing against the people or the customs of the fathers, hence the law. This combination of "people" and "law," and the order, with people (*laos*) first, is of exceptional interest.[48] Luke is the only New Testament author to speak of "sins against the people, Israel." The combination of people and law and the prominence of *laos* are important because they show that the matters of principal concern, Israel and the law, cannot be separated according to Luke. In view of the people, the law is not an independent entity but the distinguishing mark of the people of God. Luke neither understands Christianity as a "new law," [49] nor does he interpret the law as a moral law with universal validity (cf. circumcision in the formulations of the charges in 21:21).

Nomos and *laos* are inextricably connected, so that speaking against the law is speaking against the people, and speaking against the people is speaking against the law. What is meant by "sins against the people?" In no case does it mean the Gentile mission.[50] The three summaries of the Jewish charges in 21:21, 28 and 28:17, which should be viewed as a unity, show that the issue is teaching Jews not to undergo circumcision and not to live in fulfillment of the law—hence, teaching apostasy from Moses.[51] And Moses is not the moral teacher of humanity, but the teacher of Israel. Paul is therefore charged with apostasy; he is guilty of forsaking the law and is therefore no longer a member of the people of God. What provides the background for Luke's defense of Paul in 22ff. is the fact that what is at stake here is the justification of the church's existence, and along with this the salvation of the Gentiles. Yet before we deal with this in more detail, let us return to the answers which Luke gives to the charges.

In the two declarations of innocence, 25:8 and 28:17, Luke makes a direct reply. The latter, which forms the conclusion of the whole account of the trial, is the more important. Paul has done nothing against the people or the law.[52] With this declaration Luke emphasizes the main point of the speeches.

Yet the two declarations of innocence are not enough. Luke also replies indirectly. Paul appears as a witness in four speeches, whereby Luke shows on the one hand that it is impossible for Paul to have taught what he is charged with, and on the other hand that Paul is especially suited to be Israel's teacher. The charges are unfounded because—and thus we may summarize Luke's reply—Paul is a Pharisee, faithful to the law and to Scripture, and thereby also true to the hope of Israel, the resurrection.

The biographical material in the Damascus speeches which Luke had at his disposal received a very specific function in this context. On several occasions he indicates in some detail that Paul was born a Jew, raised in Jerusalem, and educated as a scribe at the feet of Gamaliel. Paul is a Pharisee, faithful to the law, who was a persecutor of Christian congregations (22:3-5 and 26:4-5, 9-11). This is not to serve, however, as a demonstration of the special mercy shown the persecutor and Pharisee at Damascus. The intervening speeches in Chapters 23 and 24 indicate the function. Paul is still a Pharisee and is still faithful to the law (23:6 and 24:14-16). This fact is stressed once again. The brief episode between Paul and the High Priest in 23:1ff. is to demonstrate that Paul is more faithful to the law than the High Priest.[53]

The description of the events leading to the Jewish plot against Paul in 24:17-21 says the same thing. Paul had come to Jerusalem to fulfill the supreme obligation of the law, alms-giving.[54] Luke notes not without reason in 24:17 that the alms are intended for the people—yet Paul is charged with speaking against the people! He is seized while fulfilling an obligation enjoined by the law, an offering in the temple (24:18). Paul, the one who had been accused of teaching against the temple, had come to Jerusalem to pray, 24:11. Thus whatever Paul was as a Pharisee, he still is as a Christian, except that now he is no longer a persecutor. Thus Luke can say that it is impossible for Paul to teach what he is charged with. To put it positively, if anyone is suited to be the teacher of Israel, it is Paul. This is what the biographical statements are intended to make clear.

But Luke is still not satisfied. This is shown by another constantly recurring theme in the speeches, the resurrection. Belief in the resurrection is characterized in 23:1ff. as a Pharisaic concern. As a Pharisee, Paul must believe in the resurrection.[55] At the same time, in 26:6, where the catchword *epaggelia* appears, the resurrection expresses the promise made to the fathers. But according to 26:7 the promise made to the fathers and the concern of the Pharisees is also a concern of all twelve tribes of the people. To attain to this is the goal of Jewish worship and practice.

Once again we have returned to the main theme: the people, the fathers, Israel. In reality, the Sadducees are outside the people, and the schism which Paul is accused of creating in 24:5 is already present. Belief in the resurrection is thus the distinguishing mark of Israel. In this context, Luke substantiates the belief neither by Jesus' resurrection nor by appeal to the eye-witness of the Twelve. He proceeds from Scripture, the promises made to the fathers, Pharisaism, and the cult of the people. Here we have a clearly polemical orientation; Paul believes everything that the law and the prophets have said (24:14).[56] What he preaches at no point goes beyond what Moses and the prophets have said about the Messiah and the future of the people (26:22f.). Luke has Paul assert on several occasions that in the final analysis, he is on trial because of belief in the resurrection (23:6; 24:21; 26:6f.; 28:20; cf. also 25:19).

The intention is clear. When Luke expressly depicts belief in the resurrection as the concern and hope of the people, he can say that by accusing Paul, his judges have placed themselves outside the people and Judaism. Paul is not an apostate; the leaders of the Jews are.[57] Paul, not his accusers, has the right to speak on behalf of the people and to represent Israel. With his knowledge of the law and his belief in the Messiah, Paul is the real Pharisee and the true Jew who has the right to serve as the teacher of Israel, as he is described in the synagogue scenes in Chapters 13-19 and finally in the scene at Rome (28:17ff.).

One component of the speeches has still received no real explanation, namely, the Damascus scenes in Chapters 22 and 26. What function do they serve? With this question we proceed to the next crucial issue: Luke's intention in the apologetic speeches.

Haenchen maintains that one should not be confused by the number of Jewish charges, since Luke's real concern is the conflict between Judaism and Christianity based on the Gentile mission.[58] According to Haenchen, the real justification for Paul's appearance as the one accused is that Luke portrays him as the great missionary to the Gentiles.[59] Thus in Chapters 22-26, Paul is really only a cipher for the Gentile mission, and Luke wants to reply to the question regarding justification of the Christian Gentile mission by pointing out that Paul, the faithful adherent to the law, had not conceived the Gentile mission on his own but was compelled to it by the Damascus event.[60] Haenchen may be correct in this view, but there are difficulties. According to the account in Acts, it is Peter who institutes the circumcision-free mission among the Gentiles, while James provides the decisive sanction (Chapters 10-11 and 15). Therefore Haenchen speaks of a renewed justification of the Gentile mission based on Jesus' direct command to Paul.[61] In other words, Chapters 22-26, viewed theologically, are in part a repetition of Chapters 10, 11 and 15.

Yet it remains to a certain extent unclear why Luke, assuming that he could deal freely with his material, has not portrayed Peter and James as accused men, but only Paul. It is further unintelligible why none of the formulated charges allude to the Gentile mission. Luke does not trace the Gentile mission back to visionary experiences, but to Scripture as the Lord opened it to the disciples, and to the command of the Lord (Luke 24:46f.; Acts 1:8, 13:47). A special revelation is required only to institute the circumcision-free form of the Gentile mission (Chapters 10-11).[62] At the same time it becomes clear that in Acts, Paul is first of all a missionary to Jews and the founder of Jewish-Christian congregations in the diaspora with Gentile-Christian "proselytes" (9:15, 20; the synagogue scenes in Chapters 13-14; 16:16ff.; and 28:17ff.).

It is completely unnecessary for Luke to furnish justification for the Gentile mission once again in Chapters 22ff. And it would be a bit strange that he would offer such justification only when Paul's work was completed.

The function of the Damascus scenes within the context of Chapters 22-26 must be explained in another way. Luke's theology and composition offer another solution. He has worked out the emergence of a restored Israel, consisting of repentant Jews who are faithful adherents to the law. They possess the distinguishing mark of the people of God, circumcision, and they live according to the law of Israel. Herein lies the significance of the Jewish character of the Jerusalem congregation as it is described in the first part of Acts. The prophecies of salvation are fulfilled to this restored Israel, and through the restored people, Gentiles receive a share in God's salvation.[63] This is how Luke conceives the identity of the church and the place of Gentile Christians.

It is quite apparent that holding such a view, Luke must face a great problem, namely, what is said and "taught" about Paul's teaching concerning the law, Moses, and the people, Israel.[64] The dominant position Paul assumes in Acts is clear enough. He is not one of the Twelve and therefore not an apostle, if one proceeds from the strictly Lukan understanding of the term; but just as little is he only a missionary with a locally confined field of work, or an insignificant outsider who can simply be ignored. Beside the twelve leaders of the restored Israel,[65] he is a missionary in the diaspora and also to the Gentiles, specially chosen and called by God. It is equally clear that for Luke, most of the churches he actually knows stem from the work of Paul. Thus on the whole he reckons with a Pauline church. It is not without reason that he has the orator Tertullus accuse Paul in his speech of being a *prōtostatēs,* a leader of the sect of the Nazarenes (24:5). The charges directed against Paul thus apply to the whole "sect," to the whole church. It too is involved in the charge of apostasy, dissertion from the chosen people.

There no longer exists any doubt, therefore, what is at stake for Luke. The issue is not legal protection on the basis of *religio licita.* Viewed from the perspective of Luke's ecclesiology, the issue is the justification of the church's existence, and indirectly a concern for the Gentile mission. Hence it is theologically of decisive importance to demonstrate the Jewish orthodoxy as well as the special status of Paul within the church. Thus the biographical elements in Chapters 22 and 26, from which Paul's Pharisaic past emerges, are interpreted in the intervening speeches in Chapters 23 and 24 as referring to Paul's present status as a Pharisee. That Luke does not need to invent these speeches out of thin air, but could make use of Pauline words and phrases handed down often in misunderstood form, is a subject in itself which we cannot consider in detail here.

The purpose of the Damascus account, then, is to show how Paul's special status in the church beside the Twelve rests on a special commission from God the Father (cf. esp. 22:14f.) —something that can be attested by a man in the synagogue at Damascus who is recognized to be devout according to the law (22:12). What is to be defended and established is not the Gentile mission, but the personal status of Paul. If the greatest segment of the Christian church stems from a Jewish apostate, then the church is not the restored Israel and likewise has no right to appeal to Israel's salvation. Luke wants to show that the Twelve and Paul represent Israel, while the unrepentant Jews no longer have a claim to the designation "Israel." [66] Luke's concern is the struggle for the right of citizenship in the people of God,[67] and it is in this context that the problem of Paul must be solved.

IV

On the basis of what has been said above, it may be possible to clarify the situation and milieu out of which Luke's account arises, as well as what the account intends and why it is necessary.

For Luke the time of the mission to the Jews is past.[68] Thus Luke's situation is no different from that of Paul. At the time of the Letter to the Romans, Paul states that Jews all over the world know the gospel (Rom. 9-11, esp. 11:18ff.); the epoch in the history of salvation, in which the "full number of the Gentiles" begins to be gathered, has dawned (Rom. 11:25).[69] For Luke, the mission to the Jews lies even further in the past. But for him and his environment it is still a problem why the church carries on no mission among the Jews.

Luke answers this question by referring to the completion of the Jewish mission by the Twelve and Paul.[70] But even if the time of the mission to the Jews is past, that does not mean that there exists no connection between the synagogue and the church—or to put it less anachronistically, between the two synagogues. The Jewish charges which Luke reports in his trial chapters reflect problems of his own milieu. Quite obviously there was some association with a Jewish environment, and it was necessary to offer some defense against charges aimed at the church which were directed particularly against

Paul and his remarks about the law. At the same time, the theological theme of the trial chapters and the special role that Paul plays in them reveals to us the inner side of Luke's milieu. I proceed in this context from the following assumptions: 1) While composing his double work Luke has in mind Christian readers. 2) He writes history to solve actual problems these readers have.

In this ecclesiastical milieu the Jewish Christians form a respected and influential element. Depicting Gentile Christians as proselytes of Jewish Christians (not their successors) and sharers in Israel's salvation would be unthinkable unless Christian Jews as the restored Israel were the foundation of the church. We are far removed from a time and a milieu such as we know from Justin, among others, where Jewish Christians are a contested and barely tolerated group in the church.[71] While Justin is concerned to defend fulfillment of the law on the part of Jewish Christians, the issue for Luke is the minimal demands that can be imposed on Gentile Christians in view of the Jewish law.[72] Only in a milieu with a Jewish-Christian stamp would such a lengthy explanation of the justification of the circumcision-free Gentile mission be required, as it is present in Chapters 10-15. And only in such a milieu where Jewish-Christians were conscious of their separation from the synagogue would the combination of the problems Israel-law be real.

It is not the case that for Luke the discussion about the law is only the echo of an earlier struggle between the church and Judaism. The place which this question assumes in the apologetic speeches makes such an understanding improbable. But for Luke and his environment, the problem of the law presents itself in a very different way than for Paul. Apart from the echo of Pauline preaching in 13:38 (cf. also the single remark of Peter in 15:10), nothing indicates that Luke knows or at all understands the view that the law causes sin and God's wrath.

But if the problem presents itself differently, it is still real in view of the charges made by Jewish neighbors. It can hardly be correct to maintain that Luke conceives the law as an entity belonging to the history of salvation because the first apostles kept it, while the turning point occurs with the apostolic decree, which releases Christians from obligation to the law.[73] For then it is not understandable why Luke places so much emphasis on Paul's continuing fidelity to the law—even into post-apostolic times.

This emphasis also extends to Paul's preaching to the Jews, in which he adheres to the fulfillment of the law. Of course Luke expresses this only indirectly and "negatively." Paul has said nothing against the law and the people; he himself lives as one who keeps the law. But because of the connection that exists between these statements and Paul's teaching activity, they cannot be understood in any other way. A charge of apostasy, an accusation of dissertion from the "empirical" Israel and Judaism, could have meaning only for a milieu of essentially Jewish-Christian stamp.[74]

And last but not least, the status of Paul! For this group, Paul is problematic. The effects of his "missionary successes" are alive and cannot be denied. His activity is in no sense forgotten, as happened already at the turn of the century. The problem is characteristically the rumors—baseless, according to Luke—concerning Paul's teaching about Israel and the law, as well as his apostasy from Judaism. But the concern is not with the law as a soteriological entity. Uncircumcised Gentiles had already been fully recognized with minimal fulfillment of the law. The problem is rather an ecclesiological one. In the restored Israel, the law must be fulfilled and the customs of the fathers preserved. If what the rumors report is true, the church cannot acknowledge Paul. This attitude witnesses to a milieu of a preponderant Jewish-Christian stamp.

Thus Luke intends to present a defense for Paul by means

of the apologetic speeches. He writes for Christian readers who are under fire from their Jewish neighbors because of Paul.

Notes

[1] On the curious ambiguity of Paul's position in Acts, his subordination to church tradition on the one hand and his special status on the other, cf. H. Flender, *St. Luke, Theologian of Redemptive History,* trans. R. H. Fuller (London: S.P.C.K., 1967), 129ff.

[2] Acts as a whole has more the character of a theological treatise in the form of a historical account than that of a piece of missionary propaganda or an edifying work intended for Christians. Luke does not preach but describes missionary activity located in the past; he describes and explains a mission among Jews and Gentiles. A survey of the various attempts to determine the theme of Luke's presentation in Acts is found in W. G. Kümmel, *Introduction to the New Testament,* trans. A. J. Mattill (Nashville: Abingdon Press, 1966) 112ff.

[3] Cf. my essay "The Problem of Traditions in Acts." Also N. A. Dahl, "Ordets Vekst," *NTT* 67 (1966) 32-46, and P. Borgen, "Von Paulus zu Lukas," *ST* 20 (1966) 140-157.

[4] M. Dibelius, *Studies in the Acts of the Apostles,* ed. H. Greeven (London: SCM Press, 1956) 149.

[5] For example, E. Haenchen, *The Acts of the Apostles,* trans. B. Noble *et. al.* (Philadelphia: Westminster Press, 1971) 693.

[6] For a representative view, cf. Haenchen, 693; also 578 and 622.

[7] W. M. L. De Wette, *Kurze Erklärung der Apostelgeschichte* (4th ed.; thoroughly revised and expanded by F. Overbeck; Leipzig: Weidmann, 1870) lxivf.

[8] Regarding this concept, cf. B. S. Easton, *Early Christianity,* 1955 = *The Purpose of Acts* (London: S.P.C.K., 1936) 41ff. Cf. also Haenchen, 693.

[9] H. Conzelmann, *Die Apostelgeschichte* (HNT VII; Tübingen: J. C. B. Mohr (Paul Siebeck), 1963) 10. According to Conzelmann, Luke has two chief concerns in his work: one is salvation history, the other, political apologetic.

[10] Haenchen, 100 and 691. Regarding Chapter 22, cf. Dibelius, 160.

[11] G. Stählin, *Die Apostelgeschichte* (NTD 5; Göttingen: Vandenhoeck und Ruprecht, 1962) 311.

[12] Haenchen, 693.

[13] Haenchen, 628f; cf. also M. Jones, *St. Paul the Orator* (London: 1910) 189. Dibelius, 172, finds in 26:2ff. an apologetic sermon intended to demonstrate that Christianity is the legitimate continuation of Judaism.

[14] Conzelmann, 10. According to J. Bihler, *Die Stephanusgeschichte* (München: Hueber, 1963), 177, the problem is not the relationship between Judaism and Christianity, but only the proper legal attitude toward the state.

[15] Kümmel, 115. Kümmel rejects the notion, however, that the concern is to demonstrate the Jewishness of Christianity with the hope of obtaining political recognition.

[16] *Ibid.* That is true not only for Kümmel, but also for most scholars who view the concluding chapters of Acts as political apologetic. This section then becomes a strange appendage which is only loosely connected, if at all, with the preceding portions of the work. Obviously one cannot insist that a biblical writing must have only one main theme; but preference should be given to any interpretation which can in an unstudied way exhibit a clear, inner coherence in the thematic of the writing. C. K. Barrett, *Luke the Historian in Recent Study* (London: Epworth, 1961) 63, properly maintains that there are passages which are intended to demonstrate the political innocence of Christianity, but that it is absurd so to interpret Acts as a whole. Haenchen, 100, argues that the apology for the Gentile mission forms the main theme; but there are difficulties in recognizing the Gentile mission as the theme of the trial chapters (cf. above, 165f.).

[17] Barrett, 63.

[18] Conzelmann, 10.

[19] For a different opinion, cf. Haenchen, 102.

[20] Paul's rescue during the uproar in the temple, 21:21ff., is likewise based on his Roman citizenship.

[21] Chapter 4:21-31 shows how Luke conceives the attainment of the right to practice religion for the church!

[22] For the following views, cf. my essay, "The Divided People of God: The Restoration of Israel and Salvation for the Gentiles."

[23] For Luke it is a history of salvation that throughout its epochs is Israel's history. I cannot follow Conzelmann, *The Theology of St. Luke,* trans. G. Buswell (New York: Harper and Row, 1960), 159,

when he speaks of the "past redemptive history of Israel." Even less do I agree with R. Bultmann, *Theology of the New Testament,* Vol. II, trans. K. Grobel (New York: Scribner's, 1955), 117: In Acts, Christ becomes "the beginning of a new history of salvation, the history of Christianity." Luke knows only one single unbroken history of salvation, and throughout its course the goal is always the same, namely the salvation of Israel and the Gentiles, those who come to share in the salvation of the people of God. Cf. "The Divided People of God," Parts III and IV. "The time of the church" signifies nothing but a new and decisive shift in the history of Israel.

[24] On the significance of the reports of Jewish mass-conversions, cf. "The Divided People of God," Parts II and III.

[25] Cf. M. Kiddle, "The Admission of the Gentiles in St. Luke's Gospel and Acts" *JTS* 36 (1935) 160-173, indicates that Luke seeks to substantiate the Gentile mission "from a Jewish point of view."

[26] The designation "the renewed Israel" or "the restored Israel" (in light of Acts 15:16f.) coincides with Luke's understanding of the church, while the designation "the new Israel" does not. Cf. my essay, "The Divided People of God," Parts III and IV; N. A. Dahl, "A People for His Name," *NTS* 4 (1957-58) 324. Among recent works which represent common opinion, cf. J. Gnilka, *Die Verstockung Israels, Is. 6:9, in der Theologie der Synoptiker,* (StANT 3; München: Köselverlag, 1961) 145: A new "people" is formed alongside the Jewish people. This occurs by means of an imperceptible process in so far as Luke has no peculiar designation for the new people. This process is imperceptible because it never occurs!

[27] H. Windisch, *Paulus und das Judentum,* (Stuttgart: 1935) 15, correctly notes that in Acts, Paul is as much a missionary to the diaspora as to the Gentiles. His primary task is the mission to the Jewish diaspora.

[28] According to 28:21, Paul is unknown to the Jews in Rome at this time—or more correctly—they have received no unfavorable reports about him. This verse is, however, intended to introduce Paul's final missionary preaching among the Jews.

[29] Scholars who advocate such an early date are cited in Kümmel, 114 and 132.

[30] Cf. also Luke 21:12ff. and 12:11 in relation to the other synoptic Gospels.

[31] Conzelmann, *Apostelgeschichte,* 137, finds that in 26:22ff. the apology is followed by a missionary appeal. But he overlooks the framework and the lack of a call to repentence. Windisch, 13, is correct: The crucial point is that the Christian kerygma is in no sense apostasy from Judaism. F. Bethge, *Die paulinischen Reden der Apostelgeschichte* (Göttingen: Vandenhoeck und Ruprecht, 1887), 171f., maintains that the apologetic speeches have the Jewish mission in view.

[32] In this context, Paul is thinking of Jews.

[33] Haenchen, 82, states somewhat vaguely that Luke's material in the apologetic speeches stems from biographies of Paul and the story of his conversion. A more precise answer can be given if one cites Paul's defense of himself in his letters. Luke was not familiar with Paul's letters but with a tradition about Paul's self-defense in the face of provocation. In such contexts Paul introduces autobiographical material, his past as a Pharisee and his present status as a Jew. For the latter, cf. Gal. 2:15; Rom. 11:1; Phil. 3:3; 2 Cor. 11:22. That this means something quite different for Paul than for Luke should not concern us in this context.

[34] There are Pauline "reminiscences" also in Acts 23:1 and 24:16 in the speech concerning Paul's conduct "in all good conscience"—the only two passages in which Luke employs the term "conscience" *(syneidēsis).*

[35] The designation "customs of the fathers," *ta ethē,* means the law, which is expressly stated in 6:13-14. How Luke understood the term more precisely, however—whether as written and/or oral Torah—does not emerge from the text.

[36] *Staseis* in this context can hardly mean anything but "dissension" or "schism," not "rebellion." Cf. above, 167.

[37] While in 21:21, the issue is what Paul has taught all (!) Jews "who are among the Gentiles," in 21:28 it is reported that he teaches "all men everywhere" against the people, etc. Based on the context, the latter must be interpreted by the former. This is confirmed by 24:5: The issue is Paul's activity among Jews "throughout the world."

[38] For Haenchen, 100, the justification of the Gentile mission is the real point of the speeches. Cf. also 327f. in regard to Acts 9.

[39] Cf. the numerous synagogue scenes in Chapters 13-14 with the description of the mixed assembly of Jews, proselytes and uncircumcised "God-fearers."

[40] Cf. my essay "The Divided People of God," Part V.

[41] On the literary technique of interruption, cf. Dibelius, 160.

[42] On the basis of what precedes, *heneka toutōn* in 26:21 cannot refer to the Gentile mission but rather to Paul's activity as a whole; within the account of the trial, it must refer above all to his teaching among Jews.

[43] Cf. especially Haenchen, 326ff.

[44] According to 26:19f., Paul began his work immediately with the preaching in Damascus and only later came to Jerusalem. Chapters 13 and 14 report of preaching "for the Jews first" at his frequent appearances in the synagogues.

[45] On 26:20, cf. Rom. 15:19. Cf. P. Borgen, 151f.

[46] Haenchen's remark, 648 on 23:28, is a bit strange: "Astonishingly the tribune has gathered from the confusion of the Sanhedrin session that Paul is politically innocent and is accused only because of theological differences of opinion (cf. 18:15!)."

[47] The meaning "dissension" is found also in 15:2; 23:7, 10. Bauer, *Lexicon,* 772, gives this meaning for 24:5 as well. For a contrary view, cf. Conzelmann and Haenchen in their commentaries on the appropriate passages.

[48] On the use of *laos* cf. N. A. Dahl, "A People for His Name," 324.

[49] Properly emphasized by Conzelmann, *Theology,* 159-160.

[50] Contrary to Haenchen, 630, who maintains that the prerogative of Israel is denied by the circumcision-free Gentile mission. However correct that may be historically, it is in any case not Luke's view.

[51] According to Haenchen, 115, Acts only hints at problems involving the law in connection with Paul, while the real object of controversy for Luke is the resurrection. Yet we cannot ignore the following: a) the problem of the law in the charges against Paul, b) the same problem in Paul's declarations of innocence, c) the description of the resurrection as a belief of the Pharisees, thus reflecting true faithfulness to Scripture and the law.

[52] The temple plays no special role in the account as a whole.

[53] Cf. the charges against Stephen in 6:13-14 (that he speaks against the holy place and the law) and the last words in Stephen's speech, in which he charges that the Jews have not kept the law (7:53). In the conflict between church and synagogue, the question who now keeps the law played a decisive role in the struggle for the right of membership in Israel. On the function of the law in Stephen's speech,

cf. M. Simon, *St. Stephen and the Hellenists in the Primitive Church* (London: Longmans, 1958) 46ff. and Bihler, 92.

[54] On the significance of almsgiving in fulfilling the law, cf. Str-B IV I, 536-558. Regarding the special emphasis Luke places on alms, cf. Luke 11:41; 12:33; Acts 9:36; 10:2, 31.

[55] Goppelt, *Judentum und Christentum im 1. und 2. Jahrhundert* (Gütersloh: Bertelsmann, 1954), 229, can scarcely be correct that according to Luke, the real representatives of Israel are not the Pharisees but the pious individuals in the exordium to the Gospel (Luke 1-2). This accords poorly with the general role of the Pharisees in Acts and the special emphasis on Paul's Pharisaism in 22-26. The pious individuals in the exordium are zealous for the law just as the "myriads" in the Jerusalem congregation (Acts 21:20).

[56] Peculiar to Luke is the emphasis on a) *everything* that the prophets have spoken (Luke 18:31; 24:25, 27, 44; Acts 24:14) and b) that *all* prophets have proclaimed Christ (Luke 24:27; Acts 3:18, 24; 10:43; cf. Luke 13:28; 11:49f.; Acts 7:52). The close connection with the death and resurrection of the Messiah demonstrates the polemical context of these utterances.

[57] Cf. the clear account in Windisch, 17.

[58] Haenchen, 629-630. Cf. also Jones, 189.

[59] Haenchen, *ibid.*

[60] *Ibid.*

[61] Haenchen, 630.

[62] Cf. my essay "The Divided People of God," Part V.

[63] Cf. "The Divided People of God," Part III.

[64] It is striking that Luke uses the verb *katēcheo* in 21:21 and 24, a term that he himself uses only in a technical sense (Luke 1:4 and Acts 18:25); the same is true for the rest of the New Testament (Rom. 2:18; 1 Cor. 14:19; Gal. 6:6). It is possible that Luke wants to say that among Jews, a systematic instruction concerning Paul is taking place. Paul represents an important piece of anti-Christian propaganda.

[65] Cf. the interesting article by K. H. Rengstorf, "Die Zuwahl des Matthias," *ST* 15 (1961), 35-67), who argues that the twelve apostles guarantee the continuity of the divine promise to Israel regarding the consummation of the people. I can discern, however, no contradiction between the "particularistic Jewish Christian" tendency Rengstorf finds in Acts 1:15-26, and Luke's own views in Acts.

[66] Conzelmann, *Apostelgeschichte,* 137: Jews must become Christians in order to remain Jews.

[67] W. Schmithals, *Paul and James* (Naperville, Ill.: Alec R. Allenson, Inc., 1965), 57f., correctly notes that Luke's special concern to depict Christianity as true Judaism has up to now not been satisfactorily explained. The schema in the history of salvation Conzelmann, *Apostelgeschichte,* 122, proposes (Israel/Jewish Christianity/Gentile Christianity) overlooks the fact that Paul, as the successor to the twelve apostles, teaches Jews strict adherence to the law in his activity and preaching as a missionary in the diaspora. Although for Luke the time of the mission to Jews is over, he does not necessarily view Jewish Christianity as belonging to the past.

[68] Haenchen, 100.

[69] Cf. J. Munck, *Paul and the Salvation of Mankind,* trans. F. Clarke (Richmond: John Knox Press, 1959) 277.

[70] Cf. my essay "The Divided People of God," Parts V and VI.

[71] Cf. Justin, *Dial.* esp. 46ff. on the status of Jewish Christians.

[72] *Ibid.*

[73] Thus Haenchen, 100; Conzelmann, *Theology,* 159ff. The remark of Goppelt, 232, is thoroughly bewildering, according to which Luke knows nothing about obligation to the law for anyone, not even for Jewish Christians. How can the fact then be explained that Acts exempts only Gentile Christians from obligation to the law? It is probably correct that Luke does not mention imposing obligation to the law on anyone because Jewish Christians in his milieu regarded obligation to the law as self-evident. Cf. also F. Overbeck, "Über das Verhältnis Justin des Märtyrers zur Apostelgeschichte," *ZWT* 15 (1872), 336: In regard to the law, Luke is completely unprincipled. He only appears to regard fulfillment of the law as obligatory for Jews.

[74] According to E. Trocmé *(Le "Livre des Actes" et l'histoire* (Paris: Presses universitaires de France 1957) 53ff.) the concern in the trial chapters is an inner church defense in the sense that Luke wants to defend Paul against judaizing accusations. Cf. the sharp rejection by Kümmel, 114.

James: The Defender of Paul

I

Acts provides little information about James, the brother of Jesus. Without the availability of other sources the reader would be puzzled about the role this person actually plays in Acts. He would not know who this James is,[1] why he is mentioned,[2] and what position he holds in the congregation in Jerusalem.[3]

Luke introduces James for the first time in Acts 12:17 by name only.[4] The uninformed reader would not be able to form an impression about him from this reference, except that he is important. It is quite impossible to infer from 12:17 that he is the leader of the congregation in Jerusalem.[5] Luke usually emphasizes the "credentials" of the Twelve, especially of Peter.[6] He struggles even more to legitimize Paul; in fact, this is the aim of large sections of Acts.[7] Concerning James, however, Luke does not worry about supplying the least bit of information to establish his legitimacy.[8]

Many people in Acts are nothing more than names. However, the reader is not in doubt that James, in spite of the silence surrounding his position, is actually a main figure for the writer of Acts, a kind of colorless celebrity.[9] He is the only character in Acts whose authority no one questions. At two of the most decisive points in Luke's account, he renders the final word in a controversy. In crisis and conflict he provides the answers to which all submit without objection (Chapters 15 and 21).

The structure of Acts itself provides the first clue as to James' significance, for Luke places him at two pivotal points in the story. Chapter 15 becomes the focal point for the main problems from Chapters 1-14. Peter and the Twelve are mentioned for the last time in Acts. James' appearance here is in no way intended to introduce him as a leader of the Jerusalem community and successor of the Twelve. Luke gives no hint of this. Furthermore, the Twelve in Acts obviously cannot have any successors because they are eschatological regents (Luke 22:29f.). The literary significance of James' speech (15:13ff.) within Acts is not confined to the controversial question dealt with at the Jerusalem meeting. The speech is both retrospective and prospective. The missionary activity which up to now has been carried on among the Jews and Gentiles (Chapters 2-14) receives its justification and confirmation in James' interpretation of Scripture. What has been accomplished fulfils the prophets' words about Israel and the nations (vv. 15ff.). At the same time Luke has James propose the apostolic decree concerning the Gentiles' obligations to the law, which settles the relationship between Jews and Gentiles. This decree determines the course of Paul's further missionary activity (16:4). From Acts 15:36 and throughout the remainder of the book Luke focuses his attention solely on Paul. The decree by James introduces this section of Acts.

The situation in 21:15-26 shows that Paul's missionary activity is concluded (cf. the farewell speech in 20:17ff.). The result of this activity is, among other things, a crisis in the relationship between Paul and Jerusalem on account of Paul's teaching among the Jews (vv. 20ff.).[10] Here also the point of view is retrospective. Once again James proposes a decisive solution. The line is drawn back not only through Paul's activity, but also to the apostolic decree (v. 25). At the same time James' proposal to Paul for the solution of his conflict with those zealous for the law introduces the concluding apologetic section of Acts (21, 27-28, 31), where everything is concentrated on Paul and the Jews.[11]

The Gentile mission, which concerns the relationship of Gentiles to the law and circumcision, and Paul's activity within this mission, are the main problems for the writer of Acts.[12] Therefore, James, by his very position in the composition, plays a role in Acts that is not commensurate with the silence surrounding his person, his power, and his priority. There can be only one explanation. For Luke's readers James is an undisputed authority, an uncontestable figure so well-known that it is unnecessary for Luke even to make the slightest mention of his credentials.[13] Luke can count on his readers' accepting James' authority without objection. And he uses James in two critical instances in his account, namely, at those very places where he could expect resistance and doubt among his readers. James' function in Acts is of primary importance in connection with Paul, whose conduct Luke must defend by writing Acts,[14] and to a lesser degree in connection with Peter, whose conduct is also not completely above suspicion (11:1ff.).

It appears that James serves as a key argument for enabling Luke's readers to acknowledge and accept Paul. Thus, Luke uses him as the principal witness in his defense of Paul.

II

As is well-known, Luke presents Christianity as authentic Judaism.[15] It is less recognized, however, that this is determined by Luke's ecclesiology. One of the essential identifying marks of the church is the Christians' fulfillment of the law.[16]

James appears at precisely those places where the church's Judaism no longer appears to be orthodox, and where the church's claim to be the restored Israel is endangered. The function of James is to guarantee that the conditions for being the restored people of God, the true Israel, have been met.[17] It is noteworthy that while Peter, others of the Twelve, and later Paul are subjected to persecution from the Jews as well as to criticism within the church, nothing of this sort is ever reported about James.

Luke can hardly be excused for not knowing about the martyrdom of James.[18] Regardless of the difficulties with the sources, there can be no doubt that the Jewish authorities bear the responsibility for his death which is the result of a religious trial. And it is striking that Luke makes no references to ecclesiastical opposition or Jewish criticism against James.[19] According to Acts it is puzzling how Paul could be accused of any disobedience to the law or of apostasy. On the other hand, what Luke has James say could provide grounds for criticism and accusations. It is a fact that in Acts Paul never attacks the law, nor does he utter even a single negative statement. James, on the other hand, makes many "liberal" statements.[20] Paul is the law-abiding Pharisee, but James stands at the border of orthodoxy. Luke is able to describe him in this way because no one would question the conservatism of James.

We shall take a closer look at the two main passages involving James. The main question before the Apostolic Council is the problem whether the Gentiles ought to be circumcised and whether they ought to keep the law of Moses (15:1, 5). It is not the Gentile mission as such that is the subject for discussion. That question was decided long ago (Luke 24:47ff.; Acts 1:8, 10-11).[21] Luke presents Judaism itself as a missionary religion with a positive attitude toward Gentiles as long as they submit to circumcision and keep the law. At the time of the Apostolic Council mission work had been carried on for

a long time with the admission of uncircumcised Gentiles.[22]
The problem with which Luke struggles is to what extent this
ecclesiastical practice is a breach of the law of Moses with the
result that the church as the restored Israel cannot lay claim
to the promises and salvation.[23]

In the vehement discussion that arises it is not Peter and
certainly not Paul, but James whose authority tips the scales
regarding the practice of the church, justifying it from "Jewish" perspectives. Already in the Cornelius episode Peter had
moved beyond what is permissible according to the law. He
visited the uncircumcised and had fellowship with them
(10:28). Therefore, he is subject to criticism by the Jerusalem
community (11:2ff.). Luke, however, does not consider this a
breach of the law of Moses. In the first place, Luke supports
this by referring to Cornelius' piety with regard to the law
(10:2, 4, 22, 35). Furthermore, he mentions that God has now
cleansed the hearts of converted Gentiles (10:28; 11:9;
15:8f.).[24] During the council explicit reference is made to the
Cornelius event in Peter's speech (15:7-9, see also vv. 14f.).
Peter, but not Paul, had the audacity to criticize the law: it is
a yoke, and the Jewish Christians have not borne it (v. 10).

The argument that Luke puts forward in Peter's speech is
not adequate because it does not solve the problems with
which Luke wrestles.[25] The final word comes from James.
The dissimilar introductions to the two speeches suggest that
Luke is emphasizing that James' speech goes beyond what
Peter has already said. Peter refers back to what the congregation already knows (v. 7), while James begins his speech
with an exhortation to listen to him (v. 14). In his speech
James refers first to Peter's statement. He gives it his authoritative approval. In v. 14 James gives an explanation of the
Cornelius event that goes beyond Peter's statement in v. 7. He
directs the whole discussion to the problem about the relation-

ship between Israel and Gentiles and thereby to the question of the law.

For James the event shows "how God first visited the Gentiles, to take out of them a people for his name" (v. 14). This episode is justified and confirmed on the basis of scriptural interpretation, namely, by prophetic utterances (vv. 16-18).[26] It is, however, not only this episode or even the Gentile mission that is established by the scriptural reference.[27] In that case the transition to v. 19 would be unexplainable. With the admission of Gentiles to the people of God, there are now two groups within this people. No doubt 14b is meant to correspond with 17: "to take out of them (= Gentiles) a people for his name" and "all the Gentiles who are called by my name." "A people of the Gentiles" is related to "the rebuilding of the dwelling of David which has fallen," the restoration of Israel (v. 16). James asserts that two groups of people exist within the church. The conversion of the Gentiles is the result of the conversion of Israel, as is demonstrated by the numerous references to Jewish mass conversions.[28]

This division of the church into two groups is the presupposition for the apostolic decree, or better yet, James' decree. The entire argument is carried by the difference between the two groups. It is presupposed that Jewish Christians keep the law; this point of view harmonizes with the account in Acts as a whole. On the other hand, Gentile Christians need not keep the law in its entirety. James supports this by appealing to Moses as a witness for his decision (v. 21). The apostolic decree is nothing but Mosaic law, which is applied to Gentiles living together with Israel.[29] Actually, Luke at this point has two authorities for the decree: Moses and James.

Most remarkable is the accentuation of James' authority in the opening remark of his interpretation of scripture: *dio egō krinō* (15:19).[30] *Egō* gives prominence to James, and *krinō* points to an independent decision by him. Each time this verb

appears in connection with the decree, it has the meaning
"resolve, decide" (16:4; 21:25). Luke never uses the verb with
the meaning "suggest, offer." The decree, however, is stated as
the decision of the apostles and elders in 15:23 and 16:4. Furthermore, 15:2 states that the controversy in Antioch should
be brought before the apostles and elders in Jerusalem; see
also v. 6: the apostles and the elders—James is not mentioned
—were gathered together to consider this matter.

These latter verses indicate that the decree has come to Luke
via tradition as an apostolic statement. Luke, on the other
hand, strengthens the decree by appeal to the authority of
James—and of Moses as well! In other words, Luke's readers
would recognize James' decree as Mosaic, since its content has
been preached "from of old" in the synagogues. It is important
to see that James attaches a critical comment about the law
(v. 19): To impose the fulfillment of the law on Gentiles
would mean to place a burden on them. Paul never makes
such a comment in Acts, and indeed such a comment would
be inconceivable for the Lukan Paul.

What is decisive for Luke is that the main responsibility for
the decree is placed on James.[31] The decree is thereby grounded
in scriptural and legal interpretation, not in an outpouring of
the Spirit. The purpose can only be to support the "Jewishness"
of the decree through the help of one man's authority whose
dedication to the law can not be questioned.[32]

Equally important is Luke's effort to show that this decree,
which has its application only in Pauline missionary territory
(16:4), is not to be attributed to Paul. He shares no responsibility for Gentiles' being exempted from details of the law.
Paul plays a very modest role in Acts 15. At the same time,
Luke is aware of the important role played by Paul and his
theology in the discussion about the Gentiles' obligation to
the law. Luke forces Paul's role as much as possible into the
background to avoid endangering the authority of the decree.

According to Acts 15:1, the controversy has arisen in the Antioch congregation. Thus it is indirectly associated with Paul's name (11:25ff.;13:1ff.; 14:26ff.). Paul and Barnabas are the first ones to side with the Gentiles (15:2) and are sent to Jerusalem to consider this question. Apart from his missionary report (15:4 and 12), Paul plays an insignificant role during the council. He makes no suggestions, has no decisive authority, and is simply sent back with the decision of the Jerusalem leaders.

The four references to the decree—twice in Chapter 15, again in 16:4 and finally in 21:25—reveal its significance for Luke. Each time the decree is mentioned it occurs in a discussion about Paul and his missionary activity. Each time we find a discussion of Jews and Gentiles regarding the question of the law of Moses: 15:19 and 20; 16:3 and 4,[33] and finally 21:21 and 25. Luke is aware that the decree is associated with Paul and is linked with his statements about the law. However, his concern is to keep Paul in the background and to bring James to the foreground. It is remarkable that in James' speech the missionary activity of Paul is not mentioned. On the contrary, James refers to Peter and the Cornelius episode (15:7, 14).[34] It looks as if Paul is not to be responsible for what Luke considers to be the theology of the early church. Furthermore, for James "signs and wonders" are not determinative (v. 12); they offer no proof, nor do Peter's words; only the prophets and Moses do.

The explanation for these features can only be that Luke's readers have little confidence in Paul. All ecclesiastical practices that could be traced back to him would fall under suspicion. The responsibility for the important theological decisions that result from Paul's activity rests on James' shoulders. Through James they are legitimized and made to agree with the law of Israel. In this manner James becomes the defender of Paul.

We must ask why Luke allows Paul to circumcize one of his co-workers immediately after the council (16:3). It is impossible to say whether Luke knew that according to the law Timothy should be considered a Jew. If he knew it, then he shows how thoroughly Jewish Paul is: for Paul an uncircumcised Jew is unthinkable. But if Luke considers Timothy a Gentile, then he shows how orthodox Paul is. The accusations raised against Paul in Acts 21:21, 28 are dismissed here as unfounded. Paul's dealing with Timothy provides an opportunity for James' actions at the council to stand out. It gives an impression of James as a "liberal," and of Paul as a legalist. The meaning of Acts 16:3 is not that Paul is acting from a tactical concern.[35] Luke presents Paul as being more legalistic than is necessary. The lengths to which Luke goes to free Paul from any kind of responsibility for the decree is apparent in Acts 21. Luke can even permit a minor inconsistency in his account, for it looks as if Paul here is made aware of the decree for the first time (21:25). The point, however, is that Luke intends to make his readers aware that Paul's own practice can be traced back to the one who for them wields a greater authority.[36]

III

The problem in 21:15-26 [37] is Paul's place within the framework of Luke's ecclesiology.[38] Paul's visit to Jerusalem precipitates a crisis in the congregation. It feels threatened by Paul's teaching in the Diaspora. The specific problem is Paul's relation to the law. He has allegedly taught Jews not to circumsize their children or observe the law (v. 21).[39] In spite of Luke's somewhat cautious formulation, no reader would doubt that the entire problem of Israel and the law is at issue. The name of James is mentioned again without any introduction in v. 18. Thus Luke makes James responsible for the following statements in the text.[40] From vv. 21 and 22 it may appear that James himself does not belong to "thousands zealous for the law."[41] But this is obviously contradicted by v. 24b and by the very proposal that James offers to solve the conflict between Paul and the legalists.

The point is that James and the elders are not among those disturbed by the information about Paul's teaching. Verse 23 shows that the rumors about Paul were actually believed by the congregation. Therefore Paul's visit creates a conflict. Luke depicts James as knowing both that the rumors are false[42] and that Paul himself lives in obedience to the law. Consequently, Paul also teaches the Jews in the Diaspora to keep the law. The problem is only to get all those zealous for the law to perceive what James already knows and thereby to declare Paul's innocence. Naturally, one may ask how the congregation could believe the rumors if James could disprove them.[43] But this question demands too much of the story.[44]

At this point Luke intertwines several concerns. In the first place, he can not minimize the problems that actually existed for Paul at this time. Paul himself refers to these problems in Romans 15:30ff. In the second place, he wishes to use James as legitimation for Paul's faithfulness to the law. In the third place, he lets Paul himself furnish a decisive proof for his orthodoxy with the help of a convincing demonstration. The report about Paul's Nazirite vow may be a tradition Luke has received. Whether it is historically reliable is immaterial since such a story could easily spring up against the background of Paul's conduct elsewhere. In the fourth place, Luke has an obvious literary need for Paul's action in the temple. It provides the transition to the trial chapters and demonstrates the baselessness of the Jewish accusations (Cf. 24:17-18 and 26:21).[45] Therefore, Luke has James offer the proposal that Paul take the Nazirite oath, and Paul becomes as zealous for the law as James.

Obviously Luke does not intend to characterize James as a

tactitian who holds that the law is of no special significance.
If so, Luke would jeopardize his ecclesiology. And for Luke,
James himself keeps the law. In v. 24 James gives the purpose
of the suggestion: ". . . all will know that there is nothing in
what they have been told about you but that you yourself live
in observance of the law." In the last conflict between Jerusalem and Paul, Luke permits James to shield the controversial
missionary with his authority.

In this pericope Paul's activity among Gentiles causes no
controversy. Therefore, it seems peculiar that the apostolic
decree is mentioned in v. 25. It enters abruptly and does not
fit in the context [46] because it is connected with what Paul
allegedly taught Jews and with his own faithfulness to the
law. It is true v. 19 contains a brief account of Paul's missionary activity among Gentiles, which elicits praise (v. 20a). But
there is no connection between v. 19 and v. 25.[47] What demands our attention is not the impression that Paul is for the
first time informed about the apostolic decree, which would
indicate a source different from that in Chapter 15. What demands attention is that the apostolic decree is bound up with
Paul's relation to the law and Israel.

The position of this verse betrays something significant for
Luke's own understanding. The apostolic decree is involved
with the problems surrounding Paul. Further, it represents a
problem primarily for Jewish Christians faithful to the law—
precisely the same situation as in Chapter 15. Luke does not
see the apostolic decree primarily as relief and liberation for
Gentile Christians. His primary concern is the problems created by the decree for Jewish Christians in their relation to
the law of Moses. It is most important to observe that in this
verse the decree is repeated with the special emphasis on the
authority standing behind it: "we have sent a letter with our
judgment;" the real authority is James. The reason that Gen-

tiles do not keep the whole law, but only parts of it, is not Paul's preaching, but James' decision.

We are therefore presented in this pericope with a church in Jerusalem consisting exclusively of people zealous for the law, a Christianity in the diaspora where Jews are taught to keep the law, and finally a Gentile Christianity that adheres to the apostolic decree. Within this framework Paul finds his place, shielded by the authority of James.

IV

James appears twice in Acts. In both cases the story focuses on Paul and on the law. Only in such a context does Luke make use of James. It appears that Luke introduces James into Acts because of problems concerning Paul. Of course, it may be said that the only place after Chapter 15 where James could be mentioned is Chapter 21, the only point in Chapters 16-28 where the Jerusalem congregation is mentioned.

However, this fails to account for the silence surrounding James in the first part of Acts. But the explanation for this ought to be quite simple. Luke knows that James is not one of the Twelve. In the first part of Acts the Twelve play a significant role as the regents of the twelve tribes of Israel. The presentation of the twelve new leaders over the restored Israel is decisive for Luke's ecclesiology.[48] James cannot be among them. He lacks the necessary credentials according to Acts 1:21f. Moreover, the faithfulness to the law of the Twelve and the whole early congregation is not a subject for doubt or criticism. James need not supply any testimony on their behalf. Only in one instance, when Peter has fellowship with the Gentile Cornelius, does a certain crisis arise (11:2). In this situation Luke permits James, in retrospect, to cast his vote (15:14).

James makes a few statements that may be interpreted as

reflecting a critical attitude toward the law. How these are to be regarded historically is not our problem, only how they fit within the framework of Acts. The "criticism" comes indirectly in James' endorsement (15:13ff.) of Peter's statement (15:10) and more directly in 15:19. It is significant that Paul makes no similar criticism in Luke's account. Each time Paul is mentioned as a critic of the law, it is characterized as a false accusation (21:21, 28) or appears within the context of Paul's declarations of innocence (25:8; 28:17). Only once does Luke permit Paul to mention the doctrine of justification (13:38-39). But neither within the context of Acts nor in isolation may this statement be interpreted as a criticism of the law. It is another question whether the statement represents a pre-Pauline understanding of justification in which justification is linked with forgiveness of sins. Elsewhere in the New Testament this understanding cannot be taken as standing in opposition to the law. However, it is a question whether 13:38f. is to be interpreted so that the law of Moses gives partial justification while the forgiveness of sins gives the rest. Finally there is a statement that lends itself especially well to an interpretation within a Jewish context: man needs God's mercy in the judgment if the works of the law do not suffice. And this cannot be understood as a criticism of the law.

However for Luke Paul is vulnerable, as Chapters 21-28 clearly show. Luke is writing for readers who view Paul with suspicion and who know rumors of his apostasy from Moses. Had the statements in 13:38-39 come from Peter or James no one could have been offended. They would not be offended according to Luke who, in spite of all obscurity in his soteriology, does not advocate righteousness through good works and is able to combine his soteriology with the emphasized Jewishness of the early church. However, when coming from Paul the statement about justification is dangerous. And this is most probably the reason why Luke has Peter and James make apparently critical comments concerning the law. What Paul says is actually far less critical than what Peter and James have said. Since the faithfulness of these two towards Israel can not be doubted, Luke expects the readers to make the same inference about Paul.

It is instructive to compare Acts' description of James with that of Paul to catch a glimpse of Luke's purpose. Paul's faithfulness to the law is emphasized to the point of monotony. He was and is a Pharisee, educated under Gamaliel (22:3ff.; 23:6; 26:4ff.). He circumcizes a co-worker (16:3), twice submits to the Nazirite oath (18:18;[49] 21:23, 26), and he advocates Jewish customs (16:21).[50] He recounts the history of Israel (13:16ff.); he prays in the temple, brings gifts to the nation and joins in the worship of the people of the twelve tribes (22:17; 24:17f.; 26:6f.). He believes everything in the law and the prophets and shares the hope of Israel (23:6; 24:14f., 21; 26:6, 23; 28:21). At no point may he be suspected of transgressing the law (23:5). Luke is obviously stressing these things as an apology for Paul. The formulated accusations from ecclesiastical and Jewish circles show that such an apology was necessary (21:21, 28).

On the other side stands James. He is responsible for the apostolic decree, and thus "liberally" inclined towards the Gentile mission and their limited obligation to the law. He can also make critical statements about the law.

It is conceivable that Luke knows of no other James than the "liberal" one. But it then becomes impossible to understand why Luke must defend Stephen as well as Paul on the points where James makes sharper statements. And it remains unexplained why Luke can permit James to appear with indisputable authority. He stands out as an authority precisely at the points where the narrative deals with the extremely sensitive issue of the law and especially Paul's relation to the law. If James were the "liberal" James, he would have been useless for Luke. But since Luke knows the "historical" James and his faithfulness to the law, and since Luke can assume that his Jewish Christian readers regard James as an incontestable authority, he can attribute to him certain daring viewpoints. James needs no defense, but he can be used in the defense of Paul.

Notes

[1] Acts does not mention that James is the brother of Jesus. Nor does Luke, in contrast to Mark 6:3 and Matt. 13:55, give any information in his Gospel about a brother of Jesus named James. A reader without additional information other than that supplied by Luke would not know that the person referred to was a brother of Jesus. On the other hand, Luke mentions three others with the name James (Luke 5:10; 6:14f.; 8:51; 9:28, 54; Acts 1:13). Two are apostles (James the brother of John and James the son of Alphaeus); the other is James the brother of Judas (Acts 1:13). Since the one apostle, James the brother of John, was killed by Herod (Acts 12:2), an uninformed reader might naturally identify the James who appears in the second part of Acts with the second apostle, James the son of Alphaeus.

[2] Luke does not indicate that the Risen Lord appeared to James, as Paul reported in 1 Cor. 15:7, an indication of the authority of James. See K. Holl, *Gesammelte Aufsätze zur Kirchengeschichte,* II, (Darmstadt: Wissenschaftliche Buchgesellschaft, 1964), 48. Either Luke did not know about the appearances to James, or he has minimized them.

[3] No title or description is connected with his name. Clearly he does not belong to the Twelve, nor is he among the elders of the congregation. Holl, 49, claims that James in Acts is included among the apostles and has become their leader. There is no basis for this in Acts, but see Gal. 1-2.

[4] See H. Conzelmann, *Die Apostelgeschichte* (HNT, VII; Tübingen: J. C. B. Mohr [Paul Siebeck], 1963), 71. James is abruptly introduced as a known figure: the comment in 12:17 belongs more to Lukan redaction than to source material. See also E. Haenchen, *The Acts of the Apostles,* trans. B. Noble, *et. al.* (Philadelphia: Westminster Press, 1971), 391. Acts 1:14 names Jesus' brothers as members of the congregation, but nothing special is said about James.

[5] Nowhere in Acts does Luke indicate that James is a congregational leader, as is claimed, for example, by Holl, 49; Conzelmann, 121; see also H. von Campenhausen, "Die Nachfolge des Jakobus," ZKG 63 (1950-51) 133ff. That James was a congregational leader has been supported by Paul's statement in Gal. 2:9 and from the account of Hegesippus in Eusebius, *H.E.* II 23:4ff. See E. Schwartz, "Zu Eusebius Kirchengeschichte," *ZNW* 4 (1903) 48-62; M. Dibelius, *Der Brief des Jakobus* (Meyer, XV; Göttingen: Vandenhoeck und Ruprecht, 1964) 13ff. On the basis of Acts 15:13ff. one might think that James was an authoritative interpreter of Scripture and a legal scholar. Luke gives no reason why James should be the spokesman for the Apostolic Council. Luke does report decisions of the Jerusalem congregation in which James is not mentioned.

[6] Luke 5:1ff.; 6:13ff.; 9:1ff.; 22:28ff.; 24:33; Acts 1, etc.

[7] Cf. "Paul: The Teacher of Israel."

[8] S. G. F. Brandon in *The Fall of Jerusalem and the Christian Church* (London: S.P.C.K., 1951) 46ff. and 110, attempts to explain the silence surrounding James in Acts. Luke is "embarrassed by the fact of James' unique prestige" and tries to keep him in the background. This is not due to Luke's view of James as a contrast to Paul and as a representative of another theology. Although this may be true for the "historical" James, it is not Luke's perspective. It is then unexplainable why James appears precisely in situations where he serves to strengthen Paul's authority.

[9] See A. Harnack, *Die Apostelgeschichte* (BENT III; Leipzig: Hinrichs, 1908) 102. In Acts, James is a figure of secondary importance. See however, p. 104 on Acts 15:13f.; ". . . in line with the book's pragmatism, he appears as highly important, in fact as decisive." See also Brandon, 46; Holl, 49.

[10] G. Kittel, "Die Stellung des Jakobus zu Judentum und Heidenchristentum," *ZNW* 30 (1931) 154f., weakens the argument that there is a conflict between Jerusalem and Paul; the conflict is between Paul and certain individuals who have reservations about him. But this does not take into account the comment that Jewish Christians are zealous for the law.

[11] Cf. "Paul: The Teacher of Israel."

[12] Cf. "Paul: The Teacher of Israel," and "The Law in Luke-Acts."

[13] Cf. Harnack, 122; E. Meyer, *Ursprung und Anfänge des Christentums* III (Stuttgart: J. G. Cotta, 1923) 223; E. Lohmeyer, *Galiläa und*

Jerusalem (Göttingen: Vandenhoeck und Ruprecht, 1936) 56f.; Brandon, 46ff.; F. J. Foakes-Jackson, *The Acts of the Apostles* (London: Harpers, 1931) 139. This is not without significance for the question of the dating of Acts; see F. J. Foakes-Jackson and Kirsopp Lake, *The Beginnings of Christianity* IV: *The Acts of the Apostles*, K. Lake and H. Cadbury (London: Macmillan, 1933) 271. Jackson claims on the basis of 21:21 that Acts is written while Jewish Christianity was still flourishing.

[14] For a more detailed presentation, see "Paul: The Teacher of Israel."

[15] For a clear presentation of this position see B. S. Easton, *The Purpose of Acts* (London: S.P.C.K., 1936).

[16] Cf. "The Law in Luke-Acts," 141-147.

[17] That James in Acts appears as principal spokesman for a "liberal" policy is claimed for example, by Brandon, 131. This can be asserted only if the statements of James are torn out of context and are not viewed in light of Luke's theology. It is especially important to see the function of James in relation to Paul. For more recent attempts to view James as a representative of a mediating attitude or a "free-minded Christianity," see Kittel, 146ff.; J. Munck, *Paul and the Salvation of Mankind* (Richmond, Virginia: John Knox Press, 1959), 69ff. and 111ff.; W. Schmithals, *Paul and James* Naperville, Ill.: Alec R. Allenson, Inc., 1965). Munck claims that it is solely through Hegesippus that we know James as a legalistic Jew (117), but the evidence does not come solely through Hegesippus. Certain comments in Josephus, *Ant.* XX 200f. ought not to be bypassed; they indicate that the distance between Hegesippus and Josephus is not as great as formerly presumed. Josephus comments that all Jews conscientious about the law dissociated themselves from the murder of James. Clearly Josephus is saying that it was a mistake to condemn James on grounds of breaking the law. The Gnostic traditions also contain obvious Jewish Christian reminiscences; see K. Rudolph, "Gnosis und Gnostizismus. Ein Forschungsbericht," *ThRu* 34 (1969) 157-160, with bibliographic references. There is no doubt that Hegesippus' account is overgrown with legend and possesses unbelievable features. Nevertheless, it cannot be dismissed as completely unhistorical as is done by Meyer, 73; Kittel, 145f., and others.

[18] Josephus, *Ant.* XX 9, 1; Hegesippus in Eusebius *H.E.* II 23:4-18.

[19] According to J. C. O'Neill, *The Theology of Acts in Its Historical Setting* (London: S.P.C.K., 1961) 74, the accusations against Stephen

for breaking the law show that Luke believes this is a common charge against Christianity in general. Christianity attacks the law. This opinion is based on Luke's omission of Mark 10:1-9 and on the charges against Paul in the last part of Acts. However, O'Neill overlooks the fact that only certain persons are accused—Jesus, Stephen, and Paul—and he fails to see that Luke presents the Jerusalem congregation so as to preclude general accusations.

[20] See above, 196f.

[21] Cf. "The Divided People of God," Part IV.

[22] Acts 11:1, 18, 20f.; 13:46ff.; 14:1, 27; 15:3, 7, 12, 14. Closely related to his theology of missions is the fact that Luke does not directly describe the missionary activity among the non-Jews, but only mentions that it takes place in connection with the synagogue. Cf. "The Divided People of God,"   .

[23] It is repeatedly pointed out that there is a striking contradiction between Chapters 11 and 15 in Acts. The mission among the Gentiles has for a long time been recognized, but nevertheless it appears that the problems connected with the mission first arise in all seriousness during the council; for a representative view see Haenchen, 462f. This probably reflects the actual historical conditions, namely, that the theological problems connected with the Gentiles' conversion was a subject for theological reflection only some time after Gentiles had been admitted. First came the actions, later the theological reflection. It is striking that all missionary activity in Acts, including the Jewish mission, begins with visionary and ecstatic experiences (2:1ff.; 8:26ff.; 9:1ff., 10-11; 13:1ff.; 22:12ff., 17ff.; 26:12ff., 19). In James' speech in Acts 15:13ff. we find this view expressed. Scripture is understood after the events have taken place.

[24] Luke is not of the opinion that the division between Jew and Gentile should be abolished (10:28). The point is that God has *now* cleansed the Gentiles' hearts by faith, that is, those Gentiles who receive the gospel, and has given them a share in Israel's salvation. Luke makes a distinction between the Gentiles who belong to the church and who live together with the restored people of God, and the remainder of the Gentiles who are still in opposition to the people of God (Acts 4:24-28; 14:16; 21:11, 28; 26:17; Luke 18:32; 21:24f. etc.). The Areopagus speech should not be cited here. This speech is not characteristic of Luke's theology as Vielhauer has claimed in "On the 'Paulinism' of Acts," *Studies in Luke-Acts,* ed. L. E. Keck and J. L.

Martyn (Nashville: Abingdon Press, 1966) 34-37. If anything in Acts is not Lukan, it is this speech, as the style as well as the large number of non-Lukan terms indicate.

[25] E. J. Epp, *The Theological Tendency of Bezae Cantabrigiensis in Acts* (Cambridge: Cambridge University Press, 1966) 104, directs attention to the manner in which D's text emphasizes Peter's authority. In v. 7 this text reads: *anestēsen en pneumati Petros kai eipen.* Peter spoke in the Spirit, but a similar claim is not made for James. D's revision of the introduction to James' speech shows that this change is not accidental. It is significant because Epp has convincingly shown that there is a marked anti-Jewish bias in D's textual revision. For D, Acts is obviously too Jewish, and D attempts to modify this feature.

[26] See A. Schlatter, *Die Apostelgeschichte* (ErNT 4; Stuttgart: Calwer, 1948) 185. The quotation from Scripture serves to ease the conscience of the Jews.

[27] For a different point of view see Haenchen, 448: "If all the Gentiles are to seek God, they ought not to be deterred by the law." Only in this way can the transition to v. 19 by "therefore" be joined to the preceding verses. However, Haenchen overlooks the fact that in the context the concern is with the Gentiles who have already sought the Lord. It is their relation to Jewish Christians that must be clarified. Viewed in this light, the connection with Chapters 10-11 is also clarified.

[28] For the meaning of mass conversions, cf. "The Divided People of God," Part II.

[29] Cf. "The Law in Luke-Acts," 143-145; see Haenchen, 449ff.; 469f.; Schmithals, 97f.; A. Loisy, *Les Actes des Apôtres* (Paris: 1920), 595.

[30] See L. Cerfaux—J. Dupont, *Les Actes des Apôtres* (Paris: 1954) on 15:19. Individual textual witnesses have tried to play down the status accorded James by this verse; the same tendency is apparent in Irenaeus, *Adv. Haer.* III. 12, 14 (17). Cf. Epp, 104. See also *The Beginnings of Christianity,* IV 177: ". . . it is the definite sentence of a judge, and the *egō* implies that he is acting by an authority which is personal." Against this Haenchen, 449 note 1, cites the actual decision made in v. 22 by the apostles, the elders, and the whole congregation. However, the decision made in v. 22 concerns the sending of a delegation to Antioch. As is claimed in *The Beginnings, krinō* can only be translated "I decide," or "I mean," but the first meaning best fits the context in Chapter 15. Acts 21:25 is also important

in this regard. James is presented as the "spokesman"; here the decree is traced back to the decisions passed by James and the elders, and there is no reference to the apostles.

[31] Schmithals, 98ff., claim that it is doubtful whether the decree has its origin among Christians and whether it has ever been acknowledged among them. The main point is that the decree has had no historical significance for the relationship between Jewish Christians and Gentile Christians. For Luke, the decree emphasizes "the Judaizing bias of the Gentile Christians" (99).

[32] It is striking how often Luke employs reliable Jews as character witnesses when he deals with questionable persons. In the only healing of a Gentile described by Luke (Luke 7:1ff.), he furnishes his source with a completely new introduction to show that from a Jewish point of view this Gentile deserves to be healed (vv. 3-5). Cornelius is attested by all the Jewish people as a pious man (Acts 10:22). Ananias' dealings with Paul are, among other things, justified in as much as he is "a devout man according to the law," acknowledged as such by all the Jews in Damascus (22:12f.). The Pharisees defend Paul's proclamation of the resurrection (23:5); cf. Gamaliel's role (5:34ff.). Luke 1-2 highlights persons surrounding Jesus who respect the law (cf. in addition, Acts 6:14). "All Jews" know of Paul's legal piety as a Pharisee (26:5; cf. 22:5). The conversion of the Samaritans is confirmed by two of those who will sit on the twelve thrones of Israel (Acts 8:14ff.).

[33] 16:4 is clearly meant to show that wherever Paul has preached and founded congregations, the decree is imposed on Gentiles. This is apparent from the connection with 15:36, which seems to indicate that there is now going to be a report of visits to Paul's congregations. However in what follows, 16:6, we are told of new missionary activity. It appears that with 15:36-16:5, Luke wants to stress the connection with the council. Because this paragraph appears before the second missionary journey, we are given the impression that Paul has in each place imposed the decision passed in Jerusalem on Gentiles. See Conzelmann, 88.

[34] Cf. M. Dibelius, *Studies in the Acts of the Apostles,* ed H. Greeven (London: SCM Press, 1956), 96f.

[35] Schmithals, 94, understands Paul's action as tactical. Paul may run into difficulties in his missionary work. Schmithals adds that this is bound up with Luke's understanding of Christianity as Judaism. But it is difficult to understand what tactical purpose is evident here. Paul

does not carry on any missionary activity in regions that he visited on earlier missionary journies. His concern (15:36ff.) is to strengthen present congregations. According to 16:2, Timothy is already accepted by the congregation in Lystra and Iconium. 16:3b may indicate that Luke is consciously describing Timothy as somewhat suspect in the eyes of Jews. Viewed in this light, Paul's action emerges as a witness to his devout faithfulness to the law. Thus the accusations against him in 21:21, 28 are invalid.

[36]An interesting comment on 21:25 is made in the manuscripts D and gig: "Concerning the believing Gentiles, they (those zealous for the law, v. 20) have no objections to raise against you, for we have decided. . . ." The point is obviously that Paul is free from any accusations of inadmissable teaching among the Gentiles. The responsibility for the decree rests on James and the elders.

[37]According to Schmithals, 85ff., the account is historically trustworthy, since Luke at this point uses a source which he reproduces. According to Schmithals, vv. 15-18 and possibly v. 19 are from "the older travel narrative," while v. 20 derives from Luke himself—"of course also on the basis of a source." It is interesting that according to Schmithals the thousands who are "zealous for the law" in v. 20 is a typically Lukan phrase. On the basis of source/redaction and historical premises Schmithals declares v. 20 unhistorical. What remains a puzzle is why Luke should write v. 20. Schmithals attempts to give an answer on p. 90: Luke writes from his conception of the church as the true Judaism. But concerning this phenomenon Schmithals writes on p. 59 that it is not "sufficiently explained." Codex D has made a significant alteration in v. 20: instead of *en tois Ioudaiois* it reads *en tē Ioudaia*. Thus the verse no longer speaks of believing Jews.

[38]Against the view that the concluding chapters in Acts are concerned with political apologetic, and also for a closer look at the relationship between Paul and the restored Israel, see "Paul: The Teacher of Israel."

[39] The many synagogue scenes with accounts of Jewish conversions give the impression that Paul is mainly a missionary to Jews. This provides a striking contrast to the missionary reports that speak of the Gentiles (14:27; 15:3, 12; 21:19). Schmithals, 89, thinks that 21:21 goes back to Luke's source, while in v. 28 we find Luke's own form of expression. It is difficult to find any basis for this. It is important

for understanding the whole pericope that "those who are zealous for the law" raise no objections against Paul's activity among Gentiles.

[40] The interpretation of James' role varies considerably in the commentaries. See for example, Th. Zahn, *Die Apostelgeschichte des Lukas* (Leipzig: Deichert, 1919-1921) II, 735: James appears as a bishop; Loisy, 793: James is merely an ornament; he plays no role at all.

[41] Attempts to remove the words *tōn pepisteukotōn* from the text lack any basis in the transmission of the text; see Munck, 239ff. These attempts do not help to clarify the text. On the contrary, an important feature of Luke's ecclesiology is lost, namely the church as the restored Israel, faithful to the law. Kittel, 154f., claims that James does not belong among those who are zealous for the law. For a more adequate view see F. F. Bruce, *The Acts of the Apostles* (London: Tyndale Press, 1952) 296.

[42] Cf. J. Weiss, *Earliest Christianity* I, ed. F. C. Grant (New York: Harper, 1959) 238, 270; A. Wickenhauser, *Die Apostelgeschichte* (RNT 5; Regensburg: F. Pustet, 1961) 239; Haenchen, 611.

[43] See Schmithals, 88ff., on the historical problems in this context.

[44] The text creates problems for the relationship between James and those who are zealous for the law only when James is not seen as a Jewish Christian faithful to the law. If James differs with the members of the congregation concerning obedience to the law, his conduct is hypocritical. If he himself is committed to faithfulness to the law, his actions become understandable. This, of course, does not remove the historical difficulty that James has not previously made it known that he has a different view of Paul than the members of the congregation seem to have; see Schmithals, 88f. This again presupposes, however, that Luke views James as the everyday leader of the congregation. But where do we find support for this in Acts? We ought to be content with the role Luke actually gives James; on important occasions he utters the final word. What Luke wants to tell his readers is simply this: the rumors about Paul are false, and James invalidates them.

[45] See "Paul: The Teacher of Israel," Part III.

[46] According to Conzelmann, 123, v. 25 is a disruption and thus belongs to the Lukan redaction; Haenchen, 610: It ". . . seems to have no connection with what precedes." Individual manuscripts have noted the problem; cf. n. 36.

[47] Haenchen, 610, links the two verses directly. After proposing how Paul should demonstrate his faithfulness to the law, James and the elders deal with the question of the Gentile Christians converted by Paul: There is no reason to be uneasy since Gentiles are placed under the four commandments. However, the text gives no indication at all that doubts were raised by anyone in regard to the Gentiles.

[48] See "The Twelve on Israel's Thrones."

[49] This must refer to Paul, and not to Aquila, as most commentators indicate.

[50] See the characteristic alteration in Codex D which has *ta ethnē* instead of *ethē*. It must be denied that Paul would have preached Jewish practices.